AMERICAN STATESMEN

EDITED BY

JOHN T. MORSE, JR.

VOL. XXII.

DOMESTIC POLITICS: THE TARIFF AND SLAVERY

JOHN C. CALHOUN

AMS PRESS
NEW YORK

J. C. Calhoun

American Statesmen

STANDARD LIBRARY EDITION

The Home of John C. Calhoun

HOUGHTON, MIFFLIN & CO.

American Statesmen

JOHN C. CALHOUN

BY

DR. H. VON HOLST

BOSTON AND NEW YORK
HOUGHTON, MIFFLIN AND COMPANY
The Riverside Press, Cambridge

Library of Congress Cataloging in Publication Data

Holst, Hermann Eduard von, 1841-1904.
  John C. Calhoun.

  (American statesmen, v. 22)
  Reprint of the 1899 ed.
  1. Calhoun, John Caldwell, 1782-1850.   I. Series.
E340.C15H72   973.5'0924 ⌈B⌉   75-128961
ISBN 0-404-50872-3

Reprinted from the edition of: 1899, Boston, New York
First AMS edition published in 1972
Manufactured in the United States of America

International Standard Book Number: 0-404-50872-3

AMS PRESS INC.
NEW YORK, N.Y.   10003

EDITOR'S PREFACE

THIS volume differs from all the other volumes
of the series in some essential characteristics.
In it the narrative element is subordinated to
other purposes, and the personal element appears hardly at all. If these traits seem to
detract from the interest of the book for the
general reader, there is at least good reason for
them. Calhoun was in fact an embodied idea;
his individuality and that idea were welded into
a single entity; his life expressed that idea,
and expressed nothing else. Correct and even
austere in his character, interested in nothing
outside of slavery, he owed such picturesqueness
as he had to the singleness of his purpose and
the intensity of his faith in the great social and
political institution of the South. But it should
be said that it was slavery as an abstraction, as
a principle, which absorbed him; as a matter of
practical business, as part of the daily affairs of
the active community, he knew and cared little
about it. The rigidity of his logic, the straight-
forwardness with which he made the journey

from his premises to his conclusions, equally
without mercy and without fear, took the place
of brilliant oratory and personal charm. Of
course he established his premises to suit himself, and he established them with infinite care,
skill, and accuracy, for he was a far-sighted
logician; but, having once settled them, he allowed nothing to tempt him aside from the road
of argument which led onward from his starting point; whithersoever that road led him he
followed it inexorably; he was always loyal to
logic. The consequence of these habits was that
Southerners did not always entirely agree with
his positions or appreciate his infallible accuracy. Even they were sometimes alarmed when
they saw the consequences and the necessities
of their own doctrines somewhat too clearly
exposed by him. But subsequent developments
and the final conclusion have demonstrated Calhoun's accurate comprehension of the political situation, and of the necessities which must
control the action of the South. Morally the
South was wrong, and physically the South
has been beaten; but intellectually events have
vindicated Calhoun's reasoning, judgment, and
political sagacity. Nevertheless, anxious as his
utterances sometimes made his followers, his followers they still remained; they could not break

away from the leadership of his forceful intellect, and for many long years, up to the time of
his death, he remained deservedly and inevitably
the chief of the Southern section. To-day the
study of his life is the study of the slaveholders'
presentation of the slavery problem. Personally
he was a striking figure in the Senate, but outside of the senate chamber there was little about
him that was of interest; there were few incidents in his life; apart from slavery, there were
few other matters which he cared about at all,
and there were absolutely none others which he
cared about much. It was because Calhoun was
thus the full and complete expression of slavery
regarded as a political and social theory that
Dr. von Holst was invited to write this volume.
With German thoroughness he has made probably the most exhaustive investigation of the
anti-slavery movement which has as yet been
made by any person along philosophical lines.
It was intended that the life of Calhoun should
present this philosophy; that it should set forth
the moral and political reasoning and the line
of argument *ex necessitate* which persuaded the
South of the righteousness of its peculiar institution, which marked out the policy which
it must pursue in order to conserve that institution, and from which it finally deduced the

destiny and the lawfulness of political separation. Precisely this task has been excellently performed. It is called the biography of a famous man, but it is in fact more properly a study of a moral, social, and political movement. It is the condensation of those principles which are illustrated by narrative and in detail in the elaborate Constitutional History which has been written by this same author.

THE EDITOR.

September, 1898.

CONTENTS

ILLUSTRATIONS

JOHN C. CALHOUN

CHAPTER I

YOUTH

LIFE is not only " stranger than fiction," but frequently also more tragical than any tragedy ever conceived by the most fervid imagination. Often in these tragedies of life there is not one drop of blood to make us shudder, nor a single event to compel the tears into the eye. A man endowed with an intellect far above the average, impelled by a high-soaring ambition, untainted by any petty or ignoble passion, and guided by a character of sterling firmness and more than common purity, yet, with fatal illusion, devoting all his mental powers, all his moral energy, and the whole force of his iron will to the service of a doomed and unholy cause, and at last sinking into the grave in the very moment when, under the weight of the top-stone, the towering pillars of the temple of his impure idol are rent to their very base, — can anything more tragical be conceived ?

That is, in a few lines, the story of the life
of John C. Calhoun. In spite of his grand career, South Carolina's greatest son has had a
more hapless fate than any other of the illus-
trious men in the history of the United States.
With few exceptions it is probable that the read-
ers of these pages will consider this a strange
or even an absurd assertion, and thereby themselves will furnish another proof of its truth.
Alexander Hamilton, America's greatest political genius, has been obliged to wait three quarters of a century to have a statue erected to his
memory, and then it had to be done by his own
offspring. Calhoun has not had to complain of
the same neglect, though nobody could have
been justly accused of ingratitude if this honor
had not been vouchsafed to him; for he has no
claims upon the gratitude of his country, although his name will forever remain one of the
foremost in its records. But, in common with
Alexander Hamilton, he is still waiting for the
only monument worthy of his memory, a biography which does him full justice; and he will
probably have to wait much longer for such a
memorial, — *œre perennius*, — which indeed, it
is not unlikely, may never be erected. As yet
it is hardly possible to pass an unbiased judgment upon him, because the wounds of the terrible conflict, in which he was during the life-

time of a whole generation the acknowledged leader, have not fully healed, and therefore those passions have not completely died away which were engendered by the catastrophe in which that conflict ended. Meanwhile, it becomes every day more difficult really to understand that struggle. Even the present generation, which has grown into manhood since the civil war, hardly realizes that it is not a soul-stirring romance, but sober history. The next generation will find it easier to form an adequate conception of the life of the ancient Indians and Egyptians than of that of their own grandfathers; for there is no other instance in all the history of the world where the civilizations of two different ages, with their antagonistic principles and modes of thinking and feeling, have been so intricately interwoven as in the United States during the times of the slavery conflict. It is only the part played by Calhoun in this conflict which puts him into the very first rank of the men who have acted on the political stage of the United States, though he has done enough else to secure for his name a permanent place in the annals of his country.

As the years roll on, the fame of Daniel Webster and Henry Clay is gradually growing dimmer, while the name of Calhoun has yet lost hardly anything of the lurid intensity with

which it glowed on the political firmament of
the United States towards the end of the first
half of this century. Nor will it ever lose
much of this. The fact is easily explained,
though it may seem strange to the superficial
student. The number of Calhoun's admirers
in his later years was insignificant in comparison with the enthusiastic hosts who knew no
more powerful charm than the captivating voice
of the eloquent Kentuckian, and to-day it will
not be seriously questioned that Webster was
intellectually more than the peer of Calhoun.
Neither of the three can lay claim to the name
of a statesman in the highest acceptation of the
term without more than one qualifying restriction, but Calhoun is certainly less entitled to it
than either of his great rivals. Moreover, these
had so many peculiar traits of character, habits,
and fancies, that their lives are a rich source of
pleasant anecdotes; and from the background
of the general historical development, their fig-
ures spring forth in bold relief with a vividness
equalling that of Washington, Jefferson, and
John Adams. Of Calhoun the man, on the
contrary, but very little is to be told. Even
his contemporaries, with perhaps the exception
of his nearest neighbors, did not know much of
his doings as a private individual, or at least
do not seem to have thought them of suffi-

cient interest to be handed down to posterity. Whether his private correspondence, which is still withheld from the public, will throw much light on this side of his life cannot be told. I have to state with regret that, according to my information, not very much is to be expected. I was assured in Charleston, by an intimate younger friend of Calhoun, that he had not been in the habit of carefully preserving his private letters, and that many of his papers, which are at present intrusted to Mr. Hunter, of Virginia, were lost during the civil war. However that may be, the newspapers of the times and the published private correspondences of his co-actors tell hardly anything of the personal relations and the home-life of the man whose slightest public act was watched with interest by the whole nation. We hear that he was a just and kind master to his slaves, that he was possessed of an uncommon conversational talent, and that he exercised an especial fascination upon young men. This is about all.

From the historical standpoint it is, of course, deeply to be regretted that we are so little informed about the every-day life of so remarkable a man; and yet one cannot help feeling at the same time a certain satisfaction that we learn no more about it. There is no better proof of the personal purity of a public man

than the complete stillness of all gossiping
tongues, among friends as well as foes. The
consequence of this silence is, however, that so
soon as the grave closes over such a public personage, the figure begins to assume a shadowy
appearance. A well-read student of the history
of the United States may often easily imagine
himself seated next to Webster and Clay at the
social board, or walking with them in the lanes
of their farms, though he may have been born
after their eyes had been closed forever. But
no one who has not actually grasped Calhoun's
hand and looked into the depth of those steady
and keen eyes will ever be tempted to indulge
for a single moment in such an illusion with
regard to him. Twenty or thirty years hence
there will not be a single person left to whom
he is or ever has been fully a man of flesh
and bone. The Representative, the Secretary
of War, the Vice-President, the "great Nullifier," the Senator, our posterity like ourselves
may be perfectly acquainted with; but the Calhoun off the political stage, the Calhoun who
ate and drank like other mortals, who laughed,
chatted, and sorrowed, who enjoyed life and bat-
tled with its small and great cares, is long ago
dead, and no pen will ever be able to recall him
to life in the same sense in which Webster and
Clay still are and will remain alive so long as

the American people cherish the memory of their great men.

Yet it is unquestionably true, as it was asserted before, that the name of Calhoun already conveys a much more definite idea to the American people than that of either Webster or Clay, and that this difference will be steadily increased in his favor. The simple explanation of this remarkable fact is, that Calhoun is in an infinitely higher degree the representative of an *idea*, and this idea is the pivotal point on which the history of the United States has turned from 1819 to nearly the end of the first century of their existence as an independent republic. From about 1830 to the day of his death, Calhoun may be called the very impersonation of the slavery question. From the moment when he assumes this character, his figure towers far above all his contemporaries, even Jackson not excepted; while up to that time he is, in spite of his uncommonly brilliant career, only an able politician of the higher and nobler order, having many peers and even a considerable number of superiors among the statesmen of the United States. These introductory remarks seem necessary in order to justify the brevity with which we are compelled to treat the youth of Calhoun and the first period of his public life.

In 1733 James Calhoun is said to have emi-
grated from Donegal in Ireland to the United
States.   He first went to Pennsylvania, then
settled on the Kanawha, in Virginia, and at
last, in 1756, removed to South Carolina.   In
1770 his son Patrick married Martha Caldwell,
the daughter of a Presbyterian emigrant from
Ireland.   John Caldwell Calhoun, the third son
of Patrick and Martha, was born March 18,
1782, in the Abbeville District, South Carolina.
Though his father died while he was still a boy,
the ardent temper of the zealous revolutionary
patriot seems to have exercised a marked influence on the formation of the character of the
son.   John remained with his mother on the
farm.   There he led a quiet and simple life, for
his father had left the family in very modest
circumstances.   No opportunity was offered him
to attend regularly a good school, and his solitary rambles in the woods had to serve in
lieu of systematic instruction.   Being from his
early childhood of a meditative turn of mind,
the youth learned to think before his memory
had become burdened with the thoughts of other
people.   This defective education in his boy-
hood made itself felt through his whole life.
In spite of the diligence with which he applied
himself later, for some years, to his books, the
stock of positive knowledge which he had to

fall back upon was never large, and the peculiar
kind of narrowness which is inseparable from
one-sidedness was among the most prominent
traits in his mental and moral structure. But
what he lacked in breadth of view he fully
made up by penetrating intensity, bold independence of thinking, and a keen instinct for
the true nature of the things which fell within
the limited circle in which his mind moved.

Calhoun had completed his eighteenth year,
when he began an uninterrupted course of systematic study in order to fit himself for the
higher walks of life. Under the direction of
his brother-in-law, Dr. Waddel, a Presbyterian
clergyman, he prepared himself for college, and
after two short years he was able to enter the
junior class at Yale. In 1804 he was graduated
with high honors, and then devoted himself for
three years to the study of law, spending eigh-
teen months of the time at the law school at
Litchfield, Connecticut. Of much more importance than the often-repeated story, that
while at Yale he had been declared fit and
likely to become some day President of the
United States, is the unmistakable fact that
his prolonged sojourn in New England exercised a marked influence upon the formation of
the political opinions which he held in the beginning of his political career.

Having returned to Abbeville, he began to practise law; but it does not appear that the public were especially eager to avail themselves of his services as an attorney and counsellor, nor that he distinguished himself in any case of importance. A man of his general ability and uncommon logical acuteness could not have failed to acquire a prominent standing in this calling if he had devoted himself to it with his whole energy. Yet he would undoubtedly never have become a great lawyer, because he was not objective enough to examine his premises with sufficient care, while he built his argument upon them with undeviating and most incisive logic, thereby frequently arriving at most shocking conclusions with nothing to stand upon except a basis of false postulates. Moreover, such natures never attain greatness, unless they pursue an aim which fills the whole head and heart with the force of a burning passion, a frame of mind into which but few men can be put by the common law; and of these few Calhoun certainly was not one. He was a born leader of men, and nature had destined him for a political career. While at college the exciting questions of the day had engrossed his whole attention, and the intelligence and earnestness with which he discussed them proved that he would try to have a hand in shaping

the events of the future. Sooner and in a
higher degree than he himself had probably
dared to anticipate, this wish was to be fulfilled.

He had barely had time to get again familiar
with the surroundings of his youth, when he
was sent by his district to the state Legislature.
The stage was too small to draw the eyes of
the nation upon the young man, but it was the
right place to prove his fitness for a larger one.
In 1811 he was elected a member of Congress,
and in the same year he married his cousin,
Floride Calhoun. She was possessed of a modest fortune, which enabled him to steer with all
sails set into the open sea of politics. On
November 4 he took his seat in the House of
Representatives, having previously removed to
Bath on the Savannah.

CHAPTER II

HOUSE OF REPRESENTATIVES

THE times were most favorable for a clever
and ambitious young statesman to make a brilliant début. The policy of commercial restrictions, with which Jefferson and Madison had
tried to force England and France to respect
the rights of neutrals, had signally failed. The
party in power had not the candor and moral
courage to acknowledge that it had stumbled
into grave mistakes, but it was apparent that
it could no more, for any length of time, pursue its old course. If the great European war
should last much longer — and there was no
prospect of its speedy termination — the United
States would evidently be forced to abandon
all half-hearted and two-edged measures, and to
adopt a clear and decisive policy. It was perhaps impossible to satisfy the commercial States;
but thus much was certain, that their dissatisfaction was too great and too well-founded to
permit an expectation that they would jog on
with impunity in the old ruts. Nor would either
the honor or the vital interests of the Union

allow that it should bow its head in meekness, and receive with folded arms the stripes which the belligerent powers were pleased to lay on its back. Whatever might be resolved upon and done, it was sure to raise a great clamor among a considerable portion of the people; yet something must be done, and in such circumstances the race generally is to the swift and the battle to the strong.

It was a coincidence of the utmost importance that the ranks of the revolutionary patriots had, by this time, become so thinned that the representatives of a new generation could grasp the helm without having to encounter the opposition of long acknowledged authority. It so happened, also, that among these newcomers on the political stage there were some exceptionally young men, possessed of a much higher order of talent than most of their seniors. So the leadership of the nation in this great crisis fell into the hands of untried and inexperienced men, who had hardly reached maturity, yet were fully conscious of their own power and worth, and who were impelled by a high-toned pride and ardent patriotism, and urged on by the glowing visions of an unbounded ambition. It was therefore to be expected that, true to the nature of hot-blooded, daring, and self-relying youth, they would ad-

vise the cutting of the Gordian knot which the
silver-haired sages of the Revolution had vainly
tried to disentangle. At which side of it, in
their opinion, the stroke of the sword should
be dealt, could not be doubtful from the first.
In spite of Napoleon, the majority of the people had not yet entirely lost the enthusiastic
sympathy awakened by the French Revolution,
and the services rendered by France to the
United States in the war of independence were
still unforgotten. On the other hand, the old
wounds which had been inflicted by the blows
exchanged with England had not quite ceased
to rankle ; the emancipated daughter smarted
under the overbearing haughtiness of the mother, whom she had once forced to submit to
her just claims. Then, too, above all else, Napoleon's violent decrees against the rights of
neutrals were to a considerable extent mere
stage lightnings, while the English Orders in
Council told with terrible effect upon the commerce and the general prosperity of the United
States, and the pretended right of visitation,
which was frequently exercised with studied
insolence, cut the American pride to the quick.
Prudential reasons of great weight might be
urged against resenting all these injuries at this
time with powder and lead, and personal interest as well as party spirit would surely put these

reasons into the strongest light.   But it was no
less certain that the passionate and indignant
appeals to the counter-reasons would awaken a
loud echo in numberless bosoms, since every
patriot had to confess to himself that they too
had great weight.

The general elections for the Twelfth Congress had resulted in favor of the war party. It
was principally due to his position towards this
overshadowing question that Henry Clay owed
his election to the speakership; and for the same
reason the Speaker awarded the second place on
the Committee on Foreign Relations to the new
member from South Carolina.   Mr. Crallé, the
editor of Calhoun's works, assures us that at
the first meeting of the members Calhoun was
— on motion of Mr. Porter, of Pennsylvania, to
whom the Speaker had assigned the chairman-
ship — unanimously chosen to preside over their
deliberations.   So he held from the first the
place which, next to the speakership, was the
most important in the House of Representatives.

On November 29, 1811, the committee, to
which that part of the President's message relating to foreign affairs had been referred, submitted its report. Although the report was
presented by Mr. Porter, it seems likely that
it was mainly written by Calhoun.   The essence
of it was contained in the following sentences : —

"To wrongs so daring in their character, and so disgraceful in their execution, it is impossible that the people of the United States should remain indifferent. We must now tamely and quietly submit, or we must resist by those means which God has placed within our reach.

"Your committee will not cast a shade on the American name by the expression of a doubt which branch of this alternative will be embraced; . . . the period has arrived when, in the opinion of your committee, it is the sacred duty of Congress to call forth the patriotism and the resources of the country."

The report concluded with six resolutions, which were designed to give effect to this opinion.

So the first act of Calhoun on the national stage was to sound the war-trumpet. Henceforth incessant war, war to the bitter end, was to be his destiny to the last day of his life; though it was in later years to be waged not against a foreign aggressor, but against internal adversaries, against the peace of the Union, against the true welfare of his own section of the country.

On December 12 Calhoun delivered his first set speech in Congress, defending the resolutions and refuting the arguments of John Randolph, who was himself a member of the Committee on Foreign Relations. On a former

occasion Calhoun had addressed to the House
a few remarks on a question of little importance, which he had concluded with an allusion
to the diffidence and embarrassment which a
young man necessarily felt in speaking to the
assembled representatives of the nation.   Now,
however, there was in his whole tone and manner no more the slightest trace of such a feeling.   He did not speak with arrogance, and
still less was there anything personally offensive in what he said, or in the manner with
which he said it.   From the beginning of his
public career he observed the parliamentary
proprieties with the rigor and naturalness of
the born gentleman.   Often did he prove that
he could wield with equal force and dexterity
the trenchant sword and the massive club, but
he always attacked the argument of his adversary and not his person, and he was never
guilty of the hectoring and bullying tone in
which so many of the Southern politicians indulged with keen relish.   From the first he
entered the lists with the proud conviction of
being fully the equal of any man, and he always spoke in the weighty tone of authority.
Upon him the shaking of Randolph's long finger made no impression.   With open visor he
met the much-dreaded antagonist, and though
he did not throw him to the ground, yet the

Virginian came out of the fight only second
best. They exchanged many a tilt, and the
ill-humor with which Randolph spoke of Calhoun, in his private correspondence, shows how
much he felt the wounds received from the
lance of that adversary.

Calhoun began his speech with the open
avowal " that the committee recommended the
measures now before the House, as a preparation for war ; " and he added, " such, in fact, was
its express resolve, agreed to, I believe by every
member, except that gentleman [Randolph].
. . . Indeed, the report could mean nothing but
war or empty menace." With lofty indignation he repelled the insinuation that, though
there was adequate cause for war, the people
would not deem their violated interests and
outraged rights of sufficient moment willingly
to defray the costs of fighting for their vindica-
tion.

" But it may be, and I believe it was said, that the
people will not pay taxes, because the rights violated
are not worth defending ; or that the defence will
cost more than the gain. Sir, I here enter my solemn protest against this low and 'calculating avarice' entering this hall of legislation. It is only
fit for shops and counting-houses ; and ought not to
disgrace the seat of power by its squalid aspect.
Whenever it touches sovereign power, the nation is

ruined. It is too short-sighted to defend itself. It is a compromising spirit, always ready to yield a part to save the residue. It is too timid to have in itself the laws of self-preservation. It is never safe but under the shield of honor. . . . Sir, I am not versed in this calculating policy; and will not, therefore, pretend to estimate in dollars and cents the value of national independence. I cannot measure in shillings and pence the misery, the stripes, and the slavery of our impressed seamen; nor even the value of our shipping, commercial, and agricultural losses under the Orders in Council and the British system of blockade."

With equal candor he answered Randolph's question, why then, if all this was so, war was not declared immediately: "Because," he said, "we are not yet prepared." That there was any danger in avowing this and, at the same time, using the threatening language employed by himself and those who shared his views, he denied; because, he said, England would never be provoked into beginning hostilities from a fear of uniting "all parties here."

After this speech the passing of the resolutions by the House could not be understood otherwise than as a formal announcement that war would be declared so soon as, in the opinion of the war party, the country should be sufficiently prepared. So far as it depended

upon the House, the great question was virtually decided, and the war party pushed vigor-
ously on towards the bloody goal. They needed
half a year more to reach it. President Madison was about the last man to long for the
laurels of "the conquering hero." His whole
character as well as his political convictions
made him exceedingly loath to gratify the
wishes of the young Hotspurs, who nevertheless dragged him along by a strong rope. As
Jefferson's Secretary of State and as President
he had advocated and pursued a policy, the
legitimate consequence of which was war. He
could not now take a decided stand against the
war party without acknowledging that this policy
had been, from beginning to end, a mistaken
one, — an avowal which no statesman will easily
make, and which, on the part of Madison, would
have been a formal renunciation of his aspirations
for a second term. That was the vise in which
he was held by the war party, and mercilessly
they screwed it tighter and tighter. In vain he
tried to conciliate them by consenting to follow
their lead; they insisted that he should assume
the full responsibility, and they would be satisfied
with nothing less.

On April 1 the President sent a message to
Congress, recommending an embargo. Mr.
Grundy said that he understood it "as a war

measure, and it was meant that it should directly lead to war," and Calhoun afterwards declared " its manifest propriety as a prelude to war." Without granting to the opposition the necessary time to develop their views, Congress, on April 4, passed the bill laying an embargo on all vessels. It was limited to sixty days solely because those who held the destiny of the country in their hands were fully resolved that it should not " be permitted to expire without any hostile measure being taken against Great Britain."

It was not due to the President that this announcement, indirectly made by Calhoun on May 6, was not fulfilled to the letter. Another message laid before Congress at length all the wrongs which the United States had suffered for so many years. " We behold," it said, " in fine, on the side of Great Britain a state of war against the United States, and on the side of the United States a state of peace towards Great Britain." Therefore it was now incumbent on Congress to decide whether force should be opposed to force. This was virtually a recommendation of war. In the name of the Committee on Foreign Relations, Calhoun presented a report to the House, advising " an immediate appeal to arms," and, at the same time, he moved that a formal declaration of war should be issued against Great Britain. On the following day

the House passed this to the third reading, after
Randolph's motion, renewed by Milnor, to open
the doors, and Stow's request to postpone the
final action to the next day, had both been rejected. Thus the majority crowned the high-
handed recklessness with which, ever since the
beginning of the session, they had bent the just
claims of the minority under their imperious
will. In later years Calhoun learned well
enough to clamor for the rights of the minority,
while he was but too apt to forget that the majority also had rights, and, above all others, the
right to rule. Perhaps the time was not far
distant when he and his associates would have
reason to rue their present abuse of power, for
the declaration of war received a majority of
only thirty votes, although the Democratic majority in the full House was seventy.

In the Senate, the defection from the party
even threatened to become fatal to the wishes
of the war party. On motion of Mr. Gregg, of
Pennsylvania, the bill providing for the declaration of war was recommitted by a majority
of four. Not until June 17 did a sufficient
number of reluctant Democrats yield to allow
the amended bill to be passed to a third reading.
The House agreed to the amendments on the
following day.

A few days after the declaration of war, the

House took up the question whether and how far the restrictive policy concerning commerce should be abandoned. The Committee on Ways and Means reported a bill for the partial suspension of the Non-Importation Act. This was not deemed sufficient relief in the States on which the mistaken policy hitherto pursued had weighed most heavily. Mr. Richardson, of Massachusetts, moved the total repeal of the whole restrictive system. The motion was not agreed to ; but when it was renewed the following day in a modified form, rendering the proposition somewhat less sweeping, the casting vote of the Speaker was required to carry the day against the opposition. For two years more the pernicious policy was persisted in.

Calhoun had separated himself on this important question from the majority. He earnestly advocated the repeal of the Non-Importation Act. His obligations as a party man he satisfied by denying that Jefferson's and Madison's policy could be justly charged with pusillanimity, — a compliment the more empty, because the closing remarks of his speech proved that he himself was not convinced of the truth of the assertion. It was a question not of motives, but of policy, and as to that he said : " The restrictive system, as a mode of resistance, and a means of obtaining redress of our wrongs, has

never been a favorite one with me." The reasons on which he supported his opinion were
sound, and the whole manner in which he treated
the subject was that of a statesman standing
on sufficiently elevated ground to take in the
whole view, and not to be misled by petty
details. On the past he bestowed but a slight
glance, very properly confining himself to the
effect which the maintenance of the old policy
would have under the altered circumstances.
From this point of view, he condemned it without qualification in measured but severe terms.
" With no small mortification," he asked those
who had supported the war, and now thought its
success dependent upon the continuation of the
Non-Importation Act, whether the war was to
be " an appendage only " of this act. " If so,
I disclaim it. It is an alarming idea to be in a
state of war, and not to rely on our courage or
energy, but on a measure of peace." The assertion that, if the Non-Importation Act should
be continued, a speedy restoration of peace
might be relied upon, he declared to be delusive
and a cause of alarm, for " it will debilitate the
springs of war. . . . We have had a peace like
a war. In the name of Heaven, let us not have
the only thing that is worse, a war like a peace."
This solemn warning was certainly not out of
place ; but if it was necessary to utter it within

a week after the declaration of war, he ought to have pondered well ere he did his best to push the country into a conflict which, whatever it might become in the course of time, was originally not a national but a party war, or rather a war of the party leaders.

This all-important point had not been soon enough taken into due consideration, either by him or his associates. This is the one great blame resting upon the war party, which even those cannot gainsay who otherwise fully approve of their course. The whole war was one uninterrupted struggle against the evil consequences of this fact. There was much truth in what Calhoun had asserted in his speech on May 6. It was, indeed, to a great extent, the second war for the liberty and independence of the United States, but it was irretrievably vitiated by its party origin. How the ambitious plans of the young leaders were dashed to pieces! Instead of Canada being conquered, the time came when Calhoun, with tears in his eyes, had to ask the assistance of Webster to pull the government out of its financial difficulties, which had come to such a climax that the worst might be apprehended. It was a deep humiliation. Yet where is the American patriot who would wish to erase these pages from the tablets of the history of the Union? Much less could any one

wish to miss them in the career of Calhoun, for
in one respect, and that the most important one,
they are the most attractive and satisfactory in
the record of his life. There is at this time
nothing of sectional prejudice and narrowness
in him. He stands on the broadest national
ground, and his political sins are mainly due to
the impatient ardor and buoyancy of his patriotism. Undoubtedly he pursues the aims of his
personal ambition with full consciousness; he
does not, however, seek its satisfaction at the
expense of the Union, but by promoting what
he is fully convinced that the interests and the
honor of his country demand. The word "nation," which Calhoun in later years struck from
the political and constitutional dictionary of the
United States as having no basis whatever to
rest upon, either in fact or in law, is at this
time frequently in his mouth. How could it be
otherwise, as the idea of it was deeply imbedded
in his heart and constantly occupying his mind?
His solicitude for the *national* interests did not
cease with the war, nor was it confined to objects
immediately connected with the war or referring
exclusively to the relations of the Union to foreign powers.

In a speech delivered January 31, 1816, on
a motion to repeal the direct tax, he drew a
sketch of his views concerning the lessons to be

derived from the experiences of the war as to the policy which the United States ought to pursue in future. The starting-point of his argument was the assertion that "future wars with England are not only possible, but . . . highly probable, — nay, that they will certainly take place," because the United States would "have to encounter British jealousy and hostility in every shape; not immediately manifested by open force or violence, perhaps, but by indirect attempts to check your growth and prosperity." He therefore deemed it necessary gradually to prepare for this emergency, not only by increasing the military forces of the Union, but also by systematically developing those germs of giant strength which Providence had bestowed upon and intrusted to the American people. "As to the species of preparation, . . . the navy most certainly, in any point of view, occupies the first place. It is the most safe, most effectual, and cheapest mode of defence." The internal strife during the war would have lost much of its bitterness, if the majority had from the first understood this obvious truth, and acted accordingly. The violation of the rights and interests of the citizens of the States, as a seafaring people, had given rise to the war, and yet the demand of the New England States to wage it principally by sea

had remained unheeded, until experience forced
the majority to acknowledge, if not in words, at
least by deeds, that for once the opposition was
not prompted exclusively by local interests and
a factional spirit. If the party had listened to
the advice of Calhoun with regard to the wishes
and complaints of the opposition, the animosity
of the Northeastern Federalists would never
have reached the pitch to which it finally came.
In the light of later events, it is one of the most
interesting facts in the life of Calhoun that, in
the course of the war, the question was for a
while seriously discussed in New England whether the people of that section should not try to
form an alliance with South Carolina against
the narrow anti-commercial policy of Virginia
and her followers.

The above-mentioned speech also contains the
first declaration in favor of internal improvements. "Let us make great permanent roads;
not, like the Romans, with views of subjecting
and ruling provinces, but for the more honorable purposes of defence, and of connecting
more closely the interests of various sections of
this great country." It is true that Calhoun's
immediate object in this is also the safety of the
country in future wars; but he is not only gratified that the building of roads will incidentally
tend towards nationalizing the Union; he urges

upon Congress the measure *because* it will have this effect. Always starting from the same point, he furthermore comes to the conclusion that the national government should bestow its protecting care upon the industrial interests of the country; and here, too, he expressly states that other reasons also should induce Congress to adopt this policy.

"In regard to the question how far manufactures ought to be fostered, it is the duty of this country, as a means of defence, to encourage its domestic industry, more especially that part of it which provides the necessary materials for clothing and defence. . . . The question relating to manufactures must not depend on the abstract principle that industry, left to pursue its own course, will find in its own interests all the encouragement that is necessary. Laying the claims of manufacturers entirely out of view, on general principles, without regard to their interests, a certain encouragement should be extended at least to our woollen and cotton manufactures."

It is remarkable that in the whole speech there is no mention whatever made of the Constitution. The thought does not enter his head that constitutional objections could possibly be raised. The reason of this is simply that the statesman has not yet been transformed into the attorney of a special cause. He proceeds, as a matter of course, from the assumption that the

first question a statesman has to ask himself is
not what is constitutional, but what is wise and
politic, unless it manifestly contravenes a provision of the Constitution, and to take it for
granted that the constitutional power exists,
until the contrary is proved. As the people
have not been created for the sake of the Constitution, but the Constitution has been established by the people to secure and further the
welfare of the people, this is the only rational
course; and it is perfectly safe, since, as every
measure is sure to meet with some opposition,
any constitutional flaw with regard to the proposition will certainly be pointed out, if it can
be discovered without the aid of a microscope
and hair-splitting sophistries of pettifogging law-
yers. Only when, instead of the national interests, the interests of the slave-holders had become
the glasses through which Calhoun viewed everything, he began to search the Constitution for
the power to do what he had once recommended
as prudent and even necessary, and then he discovered things in it which he had never dreamed
of before; nay, its general spirit underwent a
radical change in his eyes.

On January 8, 1816, Calhoun, as chairman
of the Committee on National Currency, reported a bill " to incorporate the subscribers to
the Bank of the United States." In a speech

which he delivered on February 26, in support
of the bill, he referred to the constitutional
question, but merely in order to state that it
" had been already so freely and frequently
discussed, that all had made up their minds on
it." So, according to his own statement, he had
most deliberately come to the conclusion that
Congress had the constitutional power to establish a national bank. Though this has necessarily to be inferred from the fact of his report-
ing the bill, it had to be expressly stated on
account of his subsequent attempts to make
himself and others believe that he had been compelled by the financial embarrassments of the
government to waive the constitutional question.
That these embarrassments exercised a powerful influence upon the formation of his opinions
cannot be doubted, but even in regard to the
expediency of the measure he was not solely controlled by them. " As to the question whether
a national bank would be favorable to the administration or the finances of the government,
it was one on which there was so little doubt,
that gentlemen would excuse him if he did not
enter into it." He does not say "now," or,
" under the present circumstances," but makes
a general statement without any restriction
whatever. There is nothing astonishing in this,
for the additional strength which it was sup-

posed that the national government would derive from the bank was at this time no cause of
alarm to him; and as to the other political and
economical considerations involved in the problem, he moved as yet in as thick a fog as the
whole people. The fact is, that with regard to
all the great economical problems, which were
soon to agitate the country so deeply, Calhoun
held exactly the opposite ground to that which
he afterwards occupied, on the constitutional
question as well as on that of expediency. He
and his partisans have done their very best to
invalidate the charge of inconsistency, but they
have not been able to succeed; for although an
edition of his speeches was published in which
those earlier efforts were omitted, the speeches
themselves could not be wiped from the records
of Congress, and, as was his wont, he had expressed himself too plainly and explicitly to
render the art of subsequent interpretation of
any avail. One would greatly wrong him by
doubting whether he was afterwards as sincere
as now, but his sincerity does not alter the fact
that he completely reversed his position. His
partisans have paid him a bad compliment by
asserting that his earlier utterances cannot with
fairness be called upon to bear witness against
his later doctrines, because they were but his
first impressions, put before the public without

due deliberation, in an unguarded manner, on the spur of some particular occasion. Had the House of Representatives sunk to such a bottomless depth that it followed the leadership of a young zealot who did not know how to bridle his tongue, but on the gravest questions of the day babbled out the first thoughts that happened to flit through his giddy brain? What, then, were the subjects which this chairman of most important committees seriously reflected upon, if not these, almost the only ones on which he deemed it worth his while to make long speeches? Moreover, this unpardonable levity and thoughtlessness must have lasted a long while, for he clung to these opinions for years, frequently repeating them and urging them upon Congress with increased energy.

His speech on the New Tariff Bill (April 6, 1816) was a long and carefully prepared argument in favor of the whole economical platform on which the Whig party stood to the last day of its existence. He started with the bold proposition that it was a matter of " vital importance, touching . . . the security and permanent prosperity of our country," to afford adequate protection to the cotton and woollen manufactures. Even Henry Clay and Horace Greeley have not been able to put their favorite doctrine into stronger language. Nor was he satisfied to have the fostering care of the government confined to these goods. His final aim was the industrial independence of the United States from Europe, and this, he thought, could be attained by protective duties. He bitterly complained of the unexpected "apathy and aversion" which manifested themselves on this subject. In his opinion the country was "prepared, even to maturity, for the introduction of manufactures." If he deemed it nevertheless necessary to assist them with protective duties, it was in order "to put them beyond the reach of contingency." There is not one word in the whole speech warranting the interpretation that he demands only momentary aid for the manufactures, which had been stimulated into existence by the war, and would now inevitably have to succumb to English competition, if they should not be propped up by artificial means. He advocated a "system," to which the only well-founded but not "decisive objection" was "that capital employed in manufacturing produced a greater dependence on the part of the employed than in commerce, navigation, or agriculture." Though this was to be regretted, it was "more than counterpoised" by other "incidental political advantages."

"It produced an interest strictly American, — as much so as agriculture, in which it had the decided

advantage of commerce or navigation. . . . Again, it
is calculated to bind together more closely our widely
spread republic. It will greatly increase our mutual
dependence and intercourse; and will, as a necessary
consequence, excite an increased attention to internal improvements, a subject every way so inti-
mately connected with the ultimate attainment of
national strength and the perfection of our political
institutions."

He regarded the fact that it would "make
the parts adhere more closely; that it would
form a new and most powerful cement, and out-
weigh any political objections that might be
urged against the system."

In a speech on February 4, 1817, on a bill to
set aside the bank dividends and bonus as a
permanent fund for the construction of roads
and canals, Calhoun, for the first time, entered
upon an extended argument on the constitutional question with regard to internal improvements. The objection that it is necessary to
secure the previous assent of the States, within
the limits of which the internal improvements
are to be made, he declared to be not "worth
the discussion, because the good sense of the
States may be relied on. They will, in all
cases, readily yield their assent." Also as to
the power of Congress he is so explicit that,
when he afterwards positively denied it, his

opponents need not have troubled themselves
about an argument of their own; so far as he
was concerned it would have sufficed to read
some extracts from this speech: —

"It is mainly urged that the Congress can only apply the public money in execution of the enumerated
powers. I am no advocate for refined arguments on
the Constitution. The instrument was not intended
as a thesis for the logician to exercise his ingenuity on.
[If he had but followed the example of the Persian
king, and charged his body servant to repeat to him
these two sentences every morning!] It ought to
be construed with plain good sense; and what can
be more express than the Constitution on this point?
. . . If the framers had intended to limit the use of
the money to the powers afterwards enumerated and
defined, nothing could have been more easy than to
have expressed it plainly. . . . But suppose the Constitution to be silent, why should we be confined in
the application of moneys to the enumerated powers?
There is nothing in the reason of the thing, that I
can perceive, why it should be so restricted; and the
habitual and uniform practice of the government
coincides with my opinion. . . . In reply to this uniform course of legislation, I expect it will be said
that our Constitution is founded on positive and written principles, and not on precedents. I do not deny
the position; but I have introduced these instances
to prove the uniform sense of Congress and the country (for they have not been objected to) as to our

powers; and surely they furnish better evidence of the true interpretation of the Constitution than the most refined and subtle arguments. Let it not be argued that the construction for which I contend gives a dangerous extent to the powers of Congress. In this point of view I conceive it to be more safe than the opposite. By giving a reasonable extent to the money power, it exempts us from the necessity of giving a strained and forced construction to the other enumerated powers."

Thus he was not only the champion of the constitutionality of internal improvements, but he boldly avowed latitudinarian principles with regard to the general construction of the Constitution. It was a rather remarkable coincidence that this was the last great speech which he delivered as a member of the House of Representatives. He was called to act on another stage, where less, or no, opportunity was offered to develop his views on these subjects before the whole people, but there is no proof lacking that he adhered to them for some time longer.

CHAPTER III

SECRETARY OF WAR

ALTHOUGH Calhoun, in a speech delivered on January 17, 1817, had deprecated the feeling which made "the very best talents of the House, men of the most aspiring character, anxious to fill the departments or foreign missions," he himself, less than two months afterwards, readily accepted a place in Mr. Monroe's Cabinet as Secretary of War. The duties of his office stood in no direct relation to the economical policy of the Federal government, but, as he was anxious to see his views adopted, he had no difficulty in laying them again before Congress. A resolution of the House of Representatives, of April 4, 1818, had called on him for "a plan for the application of such means as are within the power of Congress, for the purpose of opening and constructing such roads and canals as may deserve and require the aid of government, with a view to military operations in time of war." His report of January 14, 1819, began by laying down the sound and broad principle that, "a judicious system of roads and canals, constructed for the convenience of commerce and the transportation of the mail only, without any reference to military operations, is itself among the most efficient means for 'the more complete defence of the United States.' Without adverting to the fact that the roads and canals which such a system would require are, with few exceptions, precisely those which would be required for the operation of war, such a system, by consolidating our Union [!], and increasing our wealth and fiscal capacity, would add greatly to our resources in war."

He then traced in general outlines a vast plan of roads and canals, concluding his argument with the following significant remarks : —

"Many of the roads and canals which have been suggested are no doubt of the first importance to the commerce, the manufactures, the agriculture, and political prosperity of the country, but are not, for that reason, less useful or necessary for military purposes. It is, in fact, one of the great advantages of our country, enjoying so many others, that whether we regard its internal improvements in relation to military, civil, or political purposes, very nearly the same system, in all its parts, is required. . . . If those roads or canals had been pointed out which are necessary for military purposes, the list would have been small indeed."

In a report of December 3, 1824, "on the condition of the military establishment," etc.,

he recurred once more to the subject with
the same explicitness and emphasis. There is
therefore no reason to suppose Mr. Nathan
Sargent guilty of exaggeration, when he writes
that in June, 1824, " Mr. Calhoun spoke of his
projected improvements and the great benefits
that the country would derive from them with
a warmth, earnestness, and enthusiasm which
indicated that his whole soul was in ' the system ' he had projected." After he had exchanged the Secretaryship of War for the Vice-
Presidency, at a public dinner given in his
honor in the Pendleton District on April 26,
1825, the following toast was received with
great enthusiasm : " Internal improvement :
guided by the wisdom and energy of its able
advocates, it cannot fail to strengthen and perpetuate our bond of union." Again, on May
27, 1825, at Abbeville, on a similar occasion, he
himself said, " I gave my zealous efforts to all
such measures : . . . a due protection of those
manufactures of the country which had taken
root during the period of war and restrictions :
and finally, a system of connecting the various
portions of the country by a judicious system
of internal improvement." With the approval
of South Carolina, he still pointed with satisfaction and pride to his agency in promoting
what she and he were soon so decisively to con-

demn as impolitic, unjust, dangerous to the independence of the States, and unconstitutional.

In later years, Calhoun would have given much if he could have torn these leaves from his book of record as a Representative and as Secretary of War. Else these were the brightest and happiest years of his public life, though the first premonitory gusts of the storms which were to rage through all the rest of it began while he held the latter office. Many of his friends and admirers had with regret seen him abandon his seat in the legislative hall for a place in the President's council. They apprehended that he would, to a great extent, lose the renown which he had gained as a member of Congress, for they thought that the dialectic turn of his mind rendered him unfit to become a successful administrator. He undeceived them in a manner which astonished even those who had not shared these apprehensions. The Department of War was in a state of really astounding confusion when he assumed the charge of it. Into this chaos he soon brought order, and the whole service of the department received an organization so simple and at the same time so efficient that it has, in the main, been adhered to by all his successors, and proved itself capable of standing even the test of the civil war. Niles's " Register " said on March 27, 1824 : —

"Judging from the various reports that all of us have seen from the War Department, the order and harmony, regularity and promptitude, punctuality and responsibility, introduced by Mr. Calhoun in every branch of the service, have never been rivalled, and perhaps cannot be excelled ; and it must be recollected that he brought this system out of chaos. Never was the business of any department in such a state of *perfect confusion* as that now under his charge at the time when he was placed at the head of it. The open or unsettled accounts, of all sorts, must have amounted to nearly fifty millions of dollars. How great was the labor to cleanse this Augean stable ! But, mightily supported by the acute and indefatigable Mr. Hagner, the old and filthy accounts are nearly disposed of."

Calhoun himself said, with just pride, in a report to the President, " The result has been that, of the *entire amount* of money drawn from the Treasury in the year 1822 for the military service, including the pensions, amounting to $4,571,961.94, although it passed through the hands of no less than two hundred and ninety - one disbursing agents, there has not been a single defalcation, nor the loss of a cent to the government." And the principal employees of the department, in taking leave of him in a short address (February 28, 1825), bore the following testimony to his administration : —

"The degree of perfection to which you have carried the several branches of this department is believed to be without parallel. . . . From these (your personal character and private virtues) have proceeded the harmonious interchanges which have made the burden of details with which the undersigned are charged comparatively light."

Neither, on the other hand, were severe criticisms lacking. John Quincy Adams writes in his Diary : —

"The truth is that of the reforms in the War Department while he [Calhoun] was at its head, the most important was the reduction of the army from ten thousand men to six thousand men, utterly against his will, against all the influence that he could exercise, and to his entire disapprobation ; and all the other changes of organization were upon plans furnished by Generals Brown and Scott, and carried through Congress chiefly by the agency of John Williams, of Tennessee. Mr. Calhoun had no more share of mind in them than I have in the acts of Congress to which I affix my signature of approbation."

Even the most thorough examination of the records of the War Department would probably not clearly show whether and how far the latter assertion is true. For argument's sake, however, it may be granted that it is true to the letter. Would that really deprive Calhoun of all merit in the reforms ? Is it not one of the

most indispensable qualities of a statesman to
know where to go for advice, and to follow wise
counsels?

Others were not satisfied with denying that
the reforms were due to the initiative of the
Secretary. We read in the same Diary, under
date of June 2, 1822, that General D. Parker
said to the writer, "The management of the
War Department had been inefficient and extravagant, which was very susceptible of demonstration." The reproach of extravagance was
not wholly without apparent foundation. Calhoun very properly considered himself in duty
bound to advocate and promote the interests of
the army in every way not incompatible with
the true interests of the United States, and as
to these he, with equal propriety, refused to
accept the amount of money to be spent as con-
stituting the principal consideration. The best
is the cheapest, though the first outlay is larger.
In private life this maxim is nowhere better and
more commonly understood than by the people
generally in the United States. The American
politicians, however, partly for demagogical purposes and partly from honest stupidity, up to
this day but too frequently consider it an absurdity, though they are in other respects lavish
to the verge of criminality with the public money.
Calhoun fully understood that with regard to

great public interests the miser's policy is the worst extravagance. It was, perhaps, not quite so certain as Adams thought, that the reduction of the army was really a " reform," and the Secretary undoubtedly deserved much praise for taking a decided stand against those who wanted to screw down the rations and the wages of the privates, and to some extent even those of the officers, to the lowest possible point.

As to "abuses" in other respects, it is too much to say that Calhoun is absolutely blameless. In one important instance he has laid himself open to the charge of unfair dealing in the negotiation and conclusion of a treaty with an Indian tribe. Upon the whole, however, he advocated a policy towards these wards of the nation, which it would have been well for all the parties concerned to adopt and pursue with undeviating honesty. Even in our days his Indian reports might be profitably studied with regard as well to the cardinal mistakes committed in the Indian policy as to what ought to be done. To those who try to lift the responsibility for the hapless fate of the Indians from the shoulders of the American people, and allege a decree of Providence, the following testimony of Calhoun will be unsavory reading : —

" As far, however, as civilization may depend on education only, without taking into consideration the force of circumstances, it would seem that there is no insuperable difficulty in effecting the benevolent intention of the government. It may be affirmed, almost without qualification, that all the tribes within our settlements and near our borders are even solicitous for the education of their children. With the exception of the Creeks, they have everywhere freely and cheerfully assented to the establishment of schools, to which, in some instances, they have contributed. The Choctaws, in this respect, have evinced the most liberal spirit, having set aside $6000 of their amnesty in aid of the schools established among them. The reports of the teachers are almost uniformly favorable, both as to the capacity and docility of their youths. Their progress appears to be quite equal to that of white children of the same age, and they appear to be equally susceptible of acquiring habits of industry. At some of the establishments a considerable portion of the supplies are raised by the labor of the scholars and the teachers. With these indications, it would seem that there is little hazard in pronouncing that, with proper and vigorous efforts, they may receive an education equal to that of the laboring portion of our community."

Whether his theorizing propensities had anything to do with his taking such a favorable view of the capability and the desire of the Indians to raise themselves out of the darkness and sloth of their savage state need not here be inquired into. In judging this question Calhoun

was, at all events, a sufficiently matter-of-fact
man to see that, in spite of this supposed natural
capability for becoming civilized, their actual
civilization was impossible so long as the leading principle of the Indian policy hitherto pursued was not abandoned : —

"The political relation which they bear to us is by
itself of sufficient magnitude, if not removed, to prevent so desirable a state from being attained. We
have always treated them as an independent people;
and however insignificant a tribe may become, and
however surrounded by a dense white population, so
long as there are any remains it continues independent of our laws and authority. To tribes thus surrounded, nothing can be conceived more opposed to
their happiness and civilization than this state of
nominal independence. It has not one of the advantages of real independence, while it has nearly all
the disadvantages of a state of complete subjugation.
The consequence is inevitable. They lose the lofty
spirit and heroic courage of the savage state, without
acquiring the virtues which belong to the civilized.
Depressed in spirit and debauched in morals, they
dwindle away through a wretched existence, a nui-
sance to the surrounding country. Unless some system can be devised gradually to change this relation,
and with the progress of education to extend over
them our laws and authority, it is feared that all efforts to civilize them, whatever flattering appearances
they may for a time exhibit, must ultimately fail.

Tribe after tribe will sink, with the progress of our settlements and the pressure of our population, into wretchedness and oblivion. Such has been their past history, and such, without this change of political relation, it must probably continue to be."

Who would to-day venture to deny that the main error of the Americans in dealing with the Indian problem is here pointed out with the utmost clearness, and that subsequent history has fully borne out these assertions? With the same keen-sightedness with which Calhoun discerned the causes of the evil, he also found the means for its gradual cure : —

" Preparatory to so radical a change in our relation towards them, the system of education which has been adopted ought to be put into extensive and active operation. This is the foundation of all other improvements [?]. It ought gradually to be followed with a plain and simple system of laws and government, such as has been adopted by the Cherokees, a proper compression of their settlements, and a division of landed property. By introducing gradually and judiciously these improvements, they will ultimately attain such a state of intelligence, industry, and civilization as to prepare the way for a complete extension of our laws and authority over them."

It is not probable that Mr. Schurz has ever read this long-forgotten report, but whoever has been acquainted with it, and has also paid some attention to the Indian policy of Mr. Hayes's Secretary of the Interior, must have been struck by the coincidence of the views of South Carolina's great doctrinarian and of the modern "theorist," who, sixty years later, has dealt more successfully with the Indian problem than perhaps any other man.

Of the other charges brought against the management of the War Department, but one more need be mentioned, and this one because it had a long history and made considerable noise at the time. We allude to the so-called Rip-Rap contract. A government contract for the delivery of a large quantity of stones at Old Point Comfort had been awarded to a certain Elijah Mix, a man of ruined commercial reputation. Calhoun was not aware of this fact concerning Mix, and he was satisfied that the conditions agreed upon were as favorable for the government as any that could be obtained at the time; but he had awarded the contract without publicly advertising it, as the law required. This fact became known when Mix failed to fulfil his obligations, and the House of Representatives prohibited any further disbursements from the appropriation made for this purpose. This untoward occurrence was the more annoying because the chief clerk of the department, a brother-in-law of Mix, had,

with the knowledge of the Secretary, afterwards
bought a part of the contract. Calhoun had not
approved of his doing so, warning him that he
would expose himself to disagreeable insinua-
tions; but neither, on the other hand, had he
forbidden it, since it was not "illegal." After
Calhoun had become Vice-President, this story
was revived by an application from Mix for another government contract. Although his bid
was the lowest, it was refused, because the history
of the Rip-Rap contract proved him to be an
irresponsible person. In the course of these
transactions a private letter from Mix, in which
he charged Calhoun with having received a
share of the profits of the Rip-Rap job, found
its way into the press. Calhoun thereupon
(September 29, 1826) addressed a letter to the
House of Representatives, "claiming investigation by the House" "in its high character of
grand inquest of the nation," at the same time
announcing to the Senate that he would not preside over its deliberations until the vile calumny
had been duly disposed of, — two steps of doubtful propriety, and if not unconstitutional, at all
events extra-constitutional. The House of Representatives might easily find itself left with no
time at all for transacting its legitimate business, if it could be required to grant the claim
of every government official of a certain rank

for an investigation of charges privately [1] preferred by any private individual; and it would
be strange indeed if a United States official
had the right to refuse to attend to his constitutional duties because somebody had been
pleased to calumniate him. If the Vice-President might do so why not the President, the
Justices of the Supreme Court, the President
pro tempore of the Senate, the Speaker of the
House, — nay, any member of Congress? Neither of these objections was entirely overlooked
at the time, but the House nevertheless appointed
a committee of investigation. Calhoun was far
from being satisfied with its proceedings, although
the report declared, " They are unanimously of
the opinion that there are no facts which will
authorize the belief, or even suspicion, that the
Vice-President was ever interested, or that he
participated, directly or indirectly, in the profits
of any contract formed with the government
through the Department of War."

No decent person had ever doubted that such
was the case. The whole scandal was an empty
bubble, but, like every scandal, it was filled with
mal-odorous gases. Calhoun would have done
well to treat it with silent contempt, instead of

[1] Calhoun's assertion that the accusation had been accorded
a place in the official records of the Department of War was
proved to be wholly unfounded.

pricking it, for neither in Congress nor out of it
was there a lack of persons who willingly used
against him everything which they could lay
their hands on, and the old truth *semper ali-
quid hæret* applied to him as well as to any
other person. In spite of the praise bestowed
upon his administration of the War Department by all impartial men, many members of
Congress selected just this department as the
principal butt of their ill-humor. John Quincy
Adams writes on June 2, 1822, " The President had enough to do to support the Secretary
of War. He had already brought himself into
collision with both Houses of Congress by supporting him." Though these animadversions
were, in the opinion of Adams, not wholly unfounded, yet he was far from thinking them
quite justified. This latter fact is the more to
be noticed, because Adams cannot be considered
an entirely unprejudiced witness, though the
stern old man was certainly most honestly convinced that he judged his colleague with the
strictest impartiality and justice.

Adams leaves us in no doubt about the true
cause of these attacks upon Calhoun : —

" There was a time during the last session of Congress when so large a proportion of members was en-
listed for Calhoun that they had it in contemplation
to hold a caucus formally to declare him a candidate

[for the presidency]. But this prospect of success roused all Crawford's and Clay's partisans against him. The administration of his department was scrutinized with severity, sharpened by personal animosity and factious malice. Some abuses were discovered, and exposed with aggravations. Cavils were made against measures of that department in the execution of the laws, and brought the President in collision with both Houses of Congress. Crawford's newspapers commenced and have kept up a course of the most violent abuse and ribaldry against him."

The presidency was at the bottom of these acrimonious bickerings, and though Adams would never have committed the slightest conscious wrong in order to secure this prize, yet he coveted it too ardently to be favorably disposed toward a prominent rival.

The estrangement between Adams and Calhoun cannot be ascribed solely to this reason, but nobody who has the least knowledge of human nature will doubt that this must have had a great deal to do with it. When the two statesmen came into such close official relation by becoming members of Mr. Monroe's Cabinet, Adams must be considered, if we take his usual austerity and chilliness into due consideration, to have spoken almost enthusiastically of his younger colleague. On January 6, 1818, he says, " Calhoun thinks for himself, independ-

ently of all the rest [namely, the other members of the Cabinet], with sound judgment,
quick discrimination, and keen observation. He
supports his opinions, too, with powerful eloquence." For several years this good opinion
grows ever stronger : —

" Mr. Calhoun is a man of fair and candid mind,
of honorable principles, of clear and quick understanding, of cool self-possession, of enlarged philosophical views, and of ardent patriotism. He is above
all sectional and factious prejudices more than any
other statesman of this Union with whom I have ever
acted. He is more sensitive to the transient manifestations of momentary public opinion, more afraid of
the first impressions of the public opinion, than I
am."

Thus Adams wrote on October 15, 1821 ;
and again, only twenty-five months later, he
says, " Calhoun, who in all his movements of
every kind has an eye to himself ; " and on the
2d of April, 1824, " Precedent and popularity,
— this is the bent of his mind. The primary
principles involved in any public question are
the last to occur to him. What *has been done*
and what *will be said* are the Jachin and Boaz
of his argument." As Adams did not accuse
Calhoun of any special dishonorable act, this
change of opinion is certainly so great that the
explanation for it must be partly sought in the

last sentence of the following entry in his Diary
(September 5, 1831) : —

"Mr. Calhoun was a member of Mr. Monroe's
administration, and during its early part pursued a
course from which I anticipated that he would prove
an ornament and a blessing to his country. I have
been deeply disappointed in him, and now expect
nothing from him but evil. His personal relations
with me have been marked, on his part, with selfish
and cold-blooded heartlessness."

It is well known how much inclined Adams
was to charge with ingratitude and base in-
trigues those with whom his political life had
brought him into close personal contact; and
furthermore, that the real experiences which he
actually encountered in this respect were bad
enough to sour a less distrustful and sweeter
temper than his. Calhoun, too, he did not
blame without reason, and, so far as our present sources allow us to judge, by far the larger
part of the responsibility for the unkind feeling
between the two rested upon the Carolinian.
Adams's well-founded complaints against Calhoun, however, chiefly arose after the presidential contest had been decided for this time.
Calhoun professed to think that Monroe should
be succeeded by a Northern man, and declared
that, if such should be the case, his first choice
would be Adams. If he, nevertheless, vigor-

ously pushed his own candidacy, it was, as he
asserted, because he thought that of all the
prominent candidates Mr. Crawford, of Georgia,
had the best chance, and him he would oppose
to the utmost extent of his power, because he
not only had no high opinion of his talents, but
could not respect him as a man. So far as
Calhoun was concerned, the war was, indeed,
principally waged between his partisans and
those of Crawford. " As Calhoun stands most
in his [Crawford's] way," says Adams's Diary
on May 2, 1822, "the great burden of his exertions this session and the last has been against
the War Department; while Calhoun, by his
haste to get at the presidency, has made a cabal
in his favor in Congress to counteract Crawford's
cabal, and the session has been little more than
a violent struggle between them; both, however,
countenancing the insidious attacks upon the
Secretary of State."

Calhoun was thrown in this tussle with his
crafty colleague of the Treasury. The same
authority, which is unimpeachable on this question, says, Calhoun's " projected nomination for
the presidency has met with hardly any countenance throughout the Union. The principal
effect of it has been to bring out Crawford's
strength, and thus to promote the interest of
the very man whom alone he professes to op-

pose. Calhoun now feels his weakness, but is not cured of his ambition." Crawford, however, was to be still more disappointed than Calhoun, and so far as the struggle between these two is concerned it was the former infinitely more than the latter who could, with justice, be accused of double-dealing and an unfair underground warfare. Yet no sincere friend of Calhoun can look quite undismayed upon this chapter of his public life. The presidential fever, that typical disease which has proved fatal to the true glory of so many statesmen of the United States, permeated the very marrow of his bones. His ambition did not betray him into any dishonorable act, but his eye became dimmed with regard to the public weal, because, consciously or unconsciously, the fatal consideration, what effect his course would have upon his standing as a candidate, entered more or less into every question. His blind admirers, if there still be any left, will, of course, not admit the truth of this assertion, and will claim that to him, too, the celebrated saying of Henry Clay applies, that he would rather be right than be President. The cool, unbiased student will, indeed, probably come to the conclusion that there was not much difference between the two in this respect; but if there were nothing else to sustain the charge against Calhoun,

it would be sufficiently proved by the influence
which he allowed his presidential aspirations to
exercise upon his personal relations. The lofty
independence of mind and truly chivalric spirit,
which were his real nature, appear blunted. He
stoops to cover with an approving and admiring
smile a resentment which is lurking in a corner
of his heart, and on the other side to break off all
social intercourse with old and highly respected
associates, merely because others, whose good
services he wishes to secure, might not like these
connections. The champion of slavery, who, with
head erect, flashing eye, and the deep-toned voice
of solemn conviction and apostolic infallibility,
dares the whole civilized world, is every inch a
man, though a sadly mistaken one ; but the politician, who is craving with thirst for the presidency, is like Ulysses before the suitors, still a
hero, but with the beggar's rags of human frailty
and weakness covering the " divine " shoulders.

Calhoun's hopes rested mainly on his popularity in Pennsylvania, the grateful affection
of the army, and the admiration of the young
men. With them his comparative youth was
an additional claim on their support ; for it was
on account of his age that his career seemed to
shine with uncommon lustre. With his elders,
however, this was one of the principal objections against his being already put at the head

of the nation. Joseph Story wrote, on September 21, 1823, to the Hon. Ezekiel Bacon, " I have great admiration for Mr. Calhoun, and think few men have more enlarged and liberal views of the true policy of the national government. But his age, or rather his youth, at the present moment, is a formidable objection to his elevation to the chair." But even if he had stood in the beginning of the sixth instead of the fifth decade of his life, his wishes would probably not have been gratified. The whole movement in his favor was premature, and had, at this time, something artificial in it. There was, after all, nothing in his career to stir up a general enthusiasm, by means of which he might have ridden on the crest of a great popular wave over the heads of all his competitors into the White House. The mass of the people were in a sober mood, verging upon indifference. The election, therefore, turned much less upon principles or great questions of policy than upon personal predilections ; and this being the case, it soon became evident that Calhoun had no chance whatever. Even in Pennsylvania, where he owed his popularity partly to the vigor with which, in 1816, he had advocated a protective tariff, he was dropped. The Harrisburg convention nominated Jackson, but gave to Calhoun the second place on the ticket as

candidate for the vice-presidency. This was a
solution of the question with which he could be
well satisfied. If he had been from the first the
weakest candidate for the presidency, he was undoubtedly the strongest for the vice-presidency;
and as he had already been spoken of for the
first place, his election to the second would, in
the eyes of many people, give him a kind of
equitable claim to be, in due time, elevated
"to the chair." Niles's "Register" of November 6, 1824, said, "He is the only candidate in
whose favor the *people* have moved, and the
voice of the people should always be respected."
Adams had already, in the preceding February,
spoken of the "courtship of the New England
Federalists by Mr. Calhoun," and of "the newspapers set up in Massachusetts to support Mr.
Calhoun." Webster wrote to his brother Ezekiel, on March 14 of the same year, "I hope all
New England will support Mr. Calhoun for the
vice-presidency. If so, he will probably be
chosen, and that will be a great thing. He is a
true man, and will do good to the country in
that situation." Webster's hopes were not disappointed. The Jackson and the Adams parties
united on Calhoun. He received 182 of the 261
electoral votes, and among these were all the
New England votes, with the exception of those
from Connecticut and one from New Hampshire.

CHAPTER IV

As the presidential election turned out, the combination vote by which he had been chosen put Calhoun into an annoying and very embarrassing position with a view to his own presidential aspirations. Although Jackson had received a plurality of the electoral votes, Adams was elected by the House of Representatives. That the House was perfectly justified in doing this, not only by the letter, but also by the spirit of the Constitution, no person can deny who is possessed of common sense and is willing to use it. Article XII., section 1, of the Constitution would be an absurdity if the House were morally obliged to choose the person upon whom a plurality of the votes had been bestowed. Besides, to whom would the preference have to be accorded, if the person receiving the plurality of the electoral votes had not also received a plurality of the popular votes? The Jackson partisans, however, were determined to seal their ears and eyes hermetically against every suggestion of reason. They declared Adams's election to be an outrage, a rebellion of the servants against the masters, for no matter what the Constitution said and required, the "*demos krateo* principle," as Senator Benton expressed it, with a somewhat sorry display of his knowledge of Greek, had been trampled under foot. The nomination of Henry Clay, whose influence had given the decision in favor of Adams, for Secretary of State filled the cup of their wrath to overflowing. The cry of "bargain" was raised, and though it was proved over and over again to be a base calumny, it did not completely die out until long after Adams and Clay were resting in their graves.

So the two camps, to whose union in his behalf Calhoun owed his elevation, stood arrayed in deadly conflict against each other. To remain neutral between them was to put himself between anvil and hammer. But with which party was he to side? Justice pleaded for Adams, ambition spoke eloquently for Jackson. Can there be any doubt that this keenest logician, who had never been and never became a fanatic of the "*demos krateo* principle" as it was now understood by the Jackson party, took a correct view of the constitutional question? In 1837, in the debate on the bill for the admission of Michigan as a State into the Union, he very emphatically reproved his adversaries for an argument, according to which "the authority of numbers sets aside the authority of the law and the Constitution." And he added, "Need I show that such a principle goes to the entire overthrow of our constitutional government, and would subvert all social order?" But from the beginning it was evident that the majority of the people would declare for Jackson. To support Adams was therefore to postpone to a remote future, if not to renounce altogether, the realization of his wishes.

The temptation proved too strong for Calhoun. It is possible, and perhaps not unlikely, that Adams judged him too harshly in attributing everything he did and left undone to the wish of undermining the administration. Thus, for instance, it seems hardly probable that the reason for Calhoun's celebrated decision, which denied the right of the Vice-President to call a Senator to order, was really, as Adams believed, only unwillingness to check Randolph's violent abuse of the administration. There was more than enough of the doctrinarian in him to render it likely that he honestly thought this power would be, or at least could lead to, an abridgment of the liberty of speech. This much, however, is certain: that the Vice-President was far from anxious to sustain the political credit of the President;

nay, though he knew how to maintain the de-
corum of his office, he was in fact one of the
leaders of the opposition.   Mr. Nathan Sargent
relates that Calhoun had said to him in December, 1825, or January, 1826, " Such was the
manner in which it [Adams's administration]
came into power that *it must be defeated at all
hazards, regardless of its measures.*"   Charity
bids us assume that he deceived himself at the
time ; but when, instead of ardent desire, bitter
disappointment became his constant companion,
whispering its suggestions into his ear, the man
and the statesman would have been ashamed
to have this sentiment recalled to his memory.

For a while it seemed as if Calhoun had not
been betrayed by his ambition into a miscal-
culation.   In the presidential election of 1828,
Jackson carried everything before him, and
Calhoun was reëlected Vice-President by 171
electoral votes.   As it was understood that
Jackson did not intend to be a candidate for
reëlection, Calhoun was apparently more likely
than ever to reach the goal of the White House.
But in fact, so far as this wish was concerned,
his star had already passed its zenith.   The
personal relation between Jackson and Calhoun was no longer what it was supposed to
be.   On the surface the waters were still perfectly smooth, but in the hidden deep they

were agitated to a degree boding no good to either Calhoun or the country. In the formation of his Cabinet Jackson had recognized the claims of Calhoun to his consideration by inviting Mr. Branch, of North Carolina, Mr. Berrien, of Georgia, and Mr. Ingham, of Pennsylvania, to seats in it. Calhoun, however, thought himself not well treated, because — with the exception, perhaps, of Ingham — these were not the men he had wished to see in the council of the President, though they were reputed to be his fast friends. Yet this was not a cause of the breach which was soon to occur between the two men, but merely a symptom of a certain coolness and an incipient mutual distrust, antedating the inauguration of Jackson, and originating in the leading political question of the day.

In 1824 the tariff question had deeply agitated the whole country. The protectionists had carried the day, but only by a slender majority, and the opposition, especially in the plantation States, had assumed a threatening aspect. Not only the expediency and justice of a protective tariff was violently contested, but also its constitutionality was most strenuously denied. The excitement reached such a height that the "Southron" and the Columbia "Telescope" advised the calling of a congress of the opposition States.

Calhoun did not approve of the passionate way in which the question was treated. Yet in the summer of 1825 he declared at a dinner given in his honor at Augusta, Georgia, that "No one would reprobate more pointedly than myself any concerted union between States for interested or sectional objects. I would consider all such concert as against the spirit of our Constitution." The national tendencies still prevailed with him, and, as has been proved before, he had not yet forsworn the economical tenets which he had so zealously defended for years. His faith in them had, however, begun to be strongly shaken, and after he had once entered upon their reëxamination he felt compelled to become their most irreconcilable enemy.

It was no whim or "gray theory" which caused the steadily progressing consolidation of the Southern States with regard to the economical questions. Slavery, in consequence of the enormous development of the cotton culture, had become the determining principle of the whole political, economical, and social life of the Southern States, and a protective tariff was absolutely incompatible with the interests of the slave-holders. Indolence and a certain slovenliness pervaded the whole life of the South, because some kinds of honest labor — all that the

South was pleased to call " menial services " —
were dishonored by slavery; and thereby all
work, except the " living by one's wits," had
come to be looked upon more or less as a dire
necessity, instead of the blissful destiny of man.
No white man could ever lose " caste." No
matter how lazy, poor, ignorant, and depraved
he might be, yet, by virtue of the color of his
skin, he was a born member of the aristocracy,
and absolutely nothing could deprive him of
his place in it ; for the gulf which separated the
whites from the negroes could no more be
bridged over than that between heaven and hell.
As the human mind is constituted, no more
powerful incentive could be offered to the mass
of the population to sink deeper into nerveless
shiftlessness.   The middle classes are the back-
bone of every civilized community, and slavery
prevented the formation of a well-to-do, intellectual, and progressive middle class more effectually than any express law could have done.
To work one's way up from the lower strata
of society into the real aristocracy of the great
land-owners, that is the great slave-holders, was
an enterprise beset with almost insuperable
difficulties, and the spirit of the community
did not encourage the undertaking of the arduous task.   The greater the difference between
this real aristocracy and the bulk of the white

population actually was in every respect, the
more the former was forced to affect absolute
equality with the lowliest of their fellow citizens. These had to be persuaded that their
interests were identical with those of the rich
planters ; and, as they had in fact more to suffer
from the effects of slavery than the slaves themselves, this could only be accomplished by systematically instilling into them a dull self-con-
ceit and suicidal arrogance, which mistook
shreds and tatters for purple and ermine. They
looked down upon every other form of civilization with an air of contemptuous superiority,
which would have been exceedingly ludicrous
if it had not been infinitely sad. That was
an education rendering those who were cursed
with it eminently fit to listen to political discussions, and to retail the pretentious and vain
political wisdom that had been showered upon
them from the stump, in their idle neighborly
chats, but making them bad farmers, while un-
fitting them for everything but farming. The
population could never become dense, for the
slave, who had to work without the spur of
self-interest, tilled the soil, in spite of all over-
seers and whips, in a manner which, instead of
improving it, exhausted it in the shortest possible time. Those who did the work could
afford utterly to dispense with thinking, and

the one head of the master could not supply this want, nor did he, in most cases, even try to do so. More and more it became the rule that the planter lived on credit, eating up his crop before it had been harvested; and if he was rich enough to grow richer, the surplus was almost invariably invested in more land and slaves. What did it matter if the rich soil was speedily turned into a barren waste! There were boundless tracts of land of still richer soil left for him to go to, with his " hands."

In a community thus constituted there is little need of artisans, and still less of efficient and skilful ones. " The upper ten thousand " had the means to supply their wants from any distance; with the mass of the people neither the means nor the wishes extended much beyond the necessaries of life; and, finally, the claims of the slaves upon life were confined to a hut, coarse raiment, coarse food, and the coarsest agricultural implements. The artisan, however, is the necessary precursor of the manufacturer. Where the standard of civilization is too low to require a numerous class of laborers skilled in all sorts of handiwork, manufacturing on a large scale is as impossible as the putting up of the roof before the building of the walls which are to support it. Moreover, the landed aristocracy, which, under democratic forms, wielded the

whole political and social power, could not but
be averse to the development of a middle class
such as the North and all Europe — with the
exception of the southeastern parts and Russia
— had to boast of. There was, in later years,
much talking and passing of resolutions upon
the duty and necessity of bringing about the industrial and commercial development to which
the bounties of nature had evidently destined
the South. At the same time, however, the
spirit which animated those middle classes in
the North and in Europe, and which alone
made them what they were, was denounced and
abused as a deadly poison, the introduction of
which into the South was more to be feared
than the plague. And these denunciations, dictated by the instinct of self-preservation, were
but too well founded. With the building up
of commerce and the industrial pursuits, that
is, with the spreading of culture and prosperity, the delusion would inevitably vanish that
the interests of the small slave-holders and the
rest of the white population coincided with those
of the great planters. These last would have
planted abolitionism at the very doors of their
mansions, and would have invited it to the seat
of honor at their hearth-stones. Slavery doomed
the South to be and to remain an almost exclusively agricultural country, and, at the same

time, to use up at a steadily advancing rate the capital which Providence had bestowed upon her in the shape of a fertile soil and a genial climate. So long as slavery remained the dominant interest in the Southern States, they, for that very reason, had to be hostile to a home industry, if it needed to be artificially nursed into existence by high protective tariffs. Everything they needed of industrial products they were obliged to buy from elsewhere, and they of course wanted to buy where they could get the articles best and cheapest. But the protective tariffs forced them to buy inferior American goods at a higher price, or to pay for the European wares much more than their real value. We need not here inquire into the wisdom of this " American system " from a national point of view. Thus much was incontestable, that it ran counter to the immediate interest of the South, or, to speak more correctly, of the great slave-holders. Therefore, as the nature of things cannot be changed, this had to remain a " fixed fact " so long as the interests of the slave-holders held undisputed sway over the slave States. If, however, a government pursues an economical policy, which is permanently opposed to the immediate interests of a geographical section of the country, this section will never acknowledge that the policy is or

can be compatible with the true national interests.

Thus far no statesman, either south or north
of Mason and Dixon's line, had fully grasped
the question. The plantation States felt the effect of the American system, but they did not
understand the original cause of the irreconcilable
conflict of interests between the two sections
of the Union, nor was any one aware that the
conflict was irreconcilable to the fullest extent
of the word. This fact was the more obscured
because some special interests, as those of the
sugar and indigo planters, caused an alliance
between a part of the extreme South and the
protectionists; and furthermore, because the border States, in consequence of their geographical
situation and the contest between the slave-holding interest and the free-labor system, limped on
both sides. Yet it was as certain as a proposition
of Euclid that the conflict was irreconcilable,
and therefore "irrepressible," because freedom
and slavery are antagonistic ideas, acting with
equal energy upon the intellectual, political,
economical, social, and moral life of a people.
It has been truly said that "compromise is the
essence of politics;" genuine compromises,
however, can only be concluded with regard to
measures, never between principles, that is, between intellectual and moral conceptions which,

in their very essence, are the opposite poles of an idea.

In relation to the concrete question, these plain truths were, at the time, as little understood by Calhoun as by any other statesman of the country. As he was not a member of Congress during the contest which terminated in the Missouri compromise, we know but little of his position towards the slavery question at this memorable period. Enough, however, is known of it to prove that he had not as yet deeply reflected upon it. Like all the other members of Mr. Monroe's Cabinet, he admitted the constitutional right of Congress to prohibit slavery in the Territories. If he had perceived that this was the pivotal point on which the whole slavery question was ultimately to turn, and that upon its decision the existence of slavery depended, he certainly would not have done so. Not that he would have wittingly misinterpreted the Constitution, but he would have seen the whole instrument in a totally different light. Already the maintenance of slavery was, in his view, an incontestable right under the fundamental law of the land, and also it was an absolute necessity. Already it was a matter of course with him that everything else must yield to this consideration. Adams writes on February 24, 1820, in his Diary : —

" I had some conversation with Calhoun on the slave question, pending in Congress. He said he did not think it would produce a dissolution of the Union, but if it should the South would be from necessity compelled to form an alliance, offensive and defensive, with Great Britain.

" I said that would be returning to the colonial state.

" He said, Yes, pretty much, but it would be forced upon them."

Ten years after Calhoun's death the South tried the realization of this programme. Long before he had begun to concentrate the whole power of his intellect upon the examination of this problem, his unerring instinct unveiled the remote future. While the thinker and the practical statesman but just enter upon the task which was to constitute the dark glory of his life, the seer points to the end, which is to come after his own bones have been turned into dust.

It was not the territorial but the economical question which opened the eyes of Calhoun and pushed him with irresistible force into a new path, so that Adams said rather too little than too much when he declared that " his career as a statesman has been marked with a series of the most flagrant inconsistencies." But he wronged him grievously in asserting that " his opinions are the sport of every popular blast," and that he " veers round in his politics, to be always before the wind, and makes his intellect the pander of his will." If these reproaches ever had any foundation, he mastered this weakness just *while* and *because* he abjured his former political faith. Mr. Curtis most justly says, in his " Life of Daniel Webster," " Mr. Calhoun was a man of deep convictions." His veering round was gradual, because it was not done to serve some impure personal end, but was the result of an honest change in his opinions. After it had once begun, it went steadily on without pausing for a single moment, because he had taken his stand on a *principle*, and followed up the consequences of it with masterly logic and fatalistic sternness of purpose.

The tariff of 1828 gave birth to his first great political manifesto, the so-called South Carolina Exposition. The document issued by the legislature of that State does not concern us here ; we have only to deal with Calhoun's original draft of it. Nor is it now of any interest whether his economical reasoning was correct or fallacious ; only the political conclusions which he drew from his economical premises are of historical importance. The essential point of these economical premises is that, according to him, there is a *permanent* conflict of

interest with regard to the tariff policy between
the "staple States" and the rest of the Union.
The reason of this is simply that the staple
States are exclusively devoted to agriculture,
and will forever remain purely agricultural communities, because "our soil, climate, habits, and
peculiar labor are adapted" to this "our ancient
and favorite pursuit." This was the wizard's
wand which worked such an astonishing meta-
morphosis in the mind of Calhoun that one is
tempted to believe that a new man, whom we
have never met before, has stepped upon the
stage. In the beginning of his career we have
heard him praised as absolutely free from sectional prejudices; and we have seen that he, indeed, judged everything from a national point of
view, hardly deigning to answer the objections
which legal quibbles, party passion, and local
interests raised against what the welfare and the
honor of the "nation" demanded. But now he
speaks of "our political system resting on the
great principle involved in the recognized diversity of geographical interests in the community,"
and adopts this for the rest of his life as the
basis of all his political reasoning and his whole
political activity. The "Exposition" fills fifty-
six printed pages, but it does not contain a
single sentence bearing directly on the national
interest. This point is only incidentally men-

tioned, with the assertion that the pretended unconstitutional usurpation of the Federal government, which has called forth the "Exposition," seriously endangers the political morality and the liberty of the republic. The national statesman is transformed into the champion of the interests and the rights of the minority, and the reason of the change is that the minority is a geographical section with a "peculiar labor" system, which creates a "recognized diversity" of interests. His first question is no more, What ought the Federal government to do, and what has it the right to do? but, What effect has the policy of the Federal government on the staple States in their peculiar situation, and what constitutional means have they for counteracting the pernicious effects of the Federal policy? The corner-stone of the political edifice of the United States is henceforth to him no more the principle that the majority is to rule, but that the minority has the right and the power to checkmate the majority, whenever it considers the Federal laws unconstitutional; in other words, whenever different views are entertained about the powers conferred by the Constitution upon the Federal government, those of the minority were to prevail, provided it was deemed worth while to have recourse to the last "constitutional" resort.

The Articles of Confederation had been sup-
planted by the Constitution in order to render
the Union " more perfect." If this purpose
was to be fulfilled, the Union must continue to
grow more perfect, for where life is there is
also development. Either it was an illusion
that the historical destiny of the North American continent could be fulfilled by welding it
into one Union composed of many republican
commonwealths, and then the Union would,
sooner or later, fall to pieces, no matter what
the Constitution said ; or the authors of the Constitution had correctly understood the genius of
the American people, and had skilfully adapted
their work to the peculiar natural conditions
of the country, and in that event the States
would steadily go on growing together as the
parts of an organic whole, no matter what this
or that man, or even this or that section, might
be pleased to proclaim as the correct interpretation of the Constitution. Calhoun had been
so well aware of this fact that a favorite argument of his in support of the policy advocated
by him had been the favorable effect it would
have upon the " consolidation of the Union."
Now there was in the whole political dictionary
no term more abhorred by him than this. The
sovereignty of the States, in the fullest sense
of the term, is declared to be *the* essential prin-

ciple of the Union ; and it is not only asserted as an incontestable right, but also claimed as an absolute political necessity in order to protect the minority against the majority. The authority quoted for this opinion is not any section of the Constitution, but the Virginia and Kentucky resolutions, with their doctrine, that the States have the right " to interpose " when the Federal government is guilty of a usurpation, because, as there is no common judge over them, they, as the parties to the compact, have to determine for themselves whether it has been violated. This theory is brought by Calhoun into the more precise formula that each State has the right to " veto " a Federal law which it deems unconstitutional. Whether such a veto is to be an injunction against the execution of the law throughout the Union, or only in the individual State, and, in the latter case, what is to become of the principle that different Federal laws cannot prevail in different parts of the Union, we do not learn from the " Exposition." We are only told that the veto ought to be pronounced by a convention as representing the sovereignty of the State, but it is left undecided whether it might not also be done by the legislature.

Calhoun was very far from having completely killed the old national Adam in his bosom. He

therefore could not entirely suppress the feeling that, if this theory were to be put into practice, it might lead after all to very strange consequences with regard to the legislative activity
of the Federal government; nay, with regard
to the life of the Union itself. So he hastened
to show that the veto was by no means so terrible a thing as it might appear at the first
glance. In adopting the Constitution the States
had so far abandoned their sovereignty that
three fourths of them could change the compact as they pleased. If, therefore, it was desired that the Federal government should have
the contested power, it was only necessary that
three fourths of the States should say so, and
all the damage done would be that the exercising of the power had been postponed for a
while. How was it that these penetrating eyes
failed to see that the Federal legislation might
thereby be turned into a bulky machine, more
fatal to healthy political life than Juggernaut's
car to the fanatical worshippers? But leaving
this practical objection aside, how was it that
he failed to see that thereby one fourth of the
States would get the power to change the Constitution at will? Suppose — and the case might
certainly very easily happen — that the Federal
government exercises a power which has been
actually granted to it by the Constitution, and

that a State sees fit to veto the law, that the
question, as must be the case, is submitted to
all the States, and the objecting State is supported by one fourth of the whole number. Is
any dialectician sharp enough to disprove the
fact that, in such a case, the Constitution,
though not a single letter is either added or
erased, has been actually changed by one fourth
of the States, though that instrument expressly
requires the consent of at least three fourths to
effect the slightest change? Working in defence of the peculiar interests of the slave-holders with the lever of the state sovereignty, Calhoun thus begins to subvert the foundation of
the whole fabric of the Constitution.

The practical conclusion to which Calhoun
came was, "that there exists a case which
would justify the interposition of this State, in
order to compel the general government to
abandon an unconstitutional power, or to appeal to this high authority [the States] to confer it by express grant." He, however, deemed
it "advisable" "to allow time for further consideration and reflection, in the hope that a returning sense of justice on the part of the majority, when they come to reflect on the wrongs
which this and the other staple States have suffered, and are suffering, may repeal the obnoxious and unconstitutional acts, and thereby pre-

vent the necessity of interposing the veto of the State."

Daniel Webster wrote on April 10, 1833, to Mr. Perry, "In December, 1828, I became thoroughly convinced that the plan of a Southern confederacy had been received with favor by a great many of the political men of the South." If this suspicion was well founded the above-quoted sentence of the Exposition proves that Calhoun, at all events, was not privy to such a plot. He not only had no desire to force a crisis upon the country, but he had strong hopes that it would be avoided, and he plainly stated his reasons for these hopes. He was "further induced, at this time, to recommend this course, under the hope that the great political revolution, which will displace from power on the 4th of March next those who have acquired authority by setting the will of the people at defiance, and which will bring in an eminent citizen, distinguished for his services to the country and his justice and patriotism, may be followed up, under his influence, with a complete restoration of the pure principles of our government." But it is to be noted that he meant exactly what he said, neither more nor less. He *hoped* that by the influence of Andrew Jackson the protectionists would be defeated, but he did not feel quite sure of it; and if his hopes should not be realized, he had explicitly stated what, in his opinion, ought to be done. In order to leave no doubt whatever on this point, he followed up the last-mentioned sentence with the declaration that, in thus recommending delay, he wished it "to be distinctly understood that neither doubts of the rightful power of the State nor apprehension of consequences" constituted the smallest part of his motives.

Calhoun's reason for not trusting too implicitly in Jackson's influence to bring about a revolution in the economical policy of the Federal government was the double programme on which the general had been elected. In the South he had been sustained as a friend of " Southern interests," *i. e.*, as an anti-protectionist; while in New York, Pennsylvania, and the West he had been supported as the firm friend of the tariff and of internal improvements. The inaugural address touched this leading question of the day but very slightly, and with such cautious vagueness that neither party was satisfied, because neither knew what it had to expect from the new President. The first annual message, which had been looked for with keen expectation, gave no more satisfaction to either. All that could be safely inferred from it was that the President would gladly see some duties reduced, but it contained nothing to justify the hope of the South that he would, on principle, throw his whole weight into the scales against the entire protective system. Calhoun even saw a direct bid for the favor of the protectionists in the proposal to divide the expected yearly surplus among the States for the execution of internal improvements. He began to look upon the President with a certain distrust, and this feeling was fully reciprocated by Jackson. Those who had no opportunity to observe the actors closely, while the curtain was down, did not, however, become aware of the fact that an ominous disturbance in the friendly relations between the two first officers of the government had occurred, until the society of the capital had begun to become convulsed by the tragi-comical intermezzo of the Mrs. Eaton affair.

No serious historian will be expected to enter upon the details of this once celebrated case of the American *chronique scandaleuse*. It is the less necessary to do so because it in fact only helped on and accelerated the important political events, of which it has frequently been said to have been the main cause. It suffices to recall to the memory of the reader that Mrs. Eaton was reported to have had before her second marriage illicit intercourse with her present

husband, the Secretary of War, and that therefore many ladies refused to admit her into their
company. Jackson, prompted partly by his
generous temper, and partly by the bitter recol-
lections of what had been said against his own
wife, exerted all his influence to break the social
ban under which the wife of his Secretary and
personal friend had been put. The ladies, however, were not to be dictated to, and they carried the day against the victor of New Orleans.
Against the wives of the members of his Cabinet even the President's iron will was powerless, and Calhoun, the Vice-President, according
to his own statement, considered it his duty
to take the lead in this determined opposition
against the attempt to force the suspected lady
upon society. Van Buren, on the contrary, who
was a widower and led a bachelor's life, even
surpassed his wonted politeness in his treatment
of Mrs. Eaton. Jackson, however, was utterly
unable to draw the correct line between private
and public affairs whenever his feelings were en-
listed in a cause. Van Buren therefore greatly
ingratiated himself with the President by assid-
uously paying his court to Mrs. Eaton, while
Calhoun, by strictly adhering to the rigid
course of morality, which has always distinguished the family life of South Carolina, had
to pay for it by a corresponding decline in Jack-

son's good will.   Both Van Buren and Calhoun
ardently wished to succeed the general in the
presidency, and neither of them failed to see
that Jackson's favor might go far towards de-
ciding who should be the next occupant of the
White House.   Moreover, Calhoun was serving
his second term as Vice-President.   All the
precedents were against his presenting himself
once more as a candidate for reëlection, and he
justly apprehended that to return for four years
into private life might postpone the realization
of his long-deferred hopes *ad calendas Græcas*.
He was therefore most anxious that Jackson
should serve but one term, while, for the same
reason, Van Buren and his partisans were not
less zealous advocates of Jackson's reëlection.

So, while everything was yet quiet and
smooth on the surface, the mine was dug and
charged; one spark sufficed to lead to a great
catastrophe.   Calhoun himself remained to the
end of his life firmly convinced that Van Buren
was the engineer who had constructed the ingenious battery for the explosion.   Though
there is no documentary proof for it, yet it can
hardly be doubted that Van Buren did in fact
take part in devising the scheme; but he was
too wary and too cunning in such transactions
ever to do himself what could be done as well,
or even better, by some devoted friend.   Ad-

ams, however, writes on January 30, 1831,
" Wirt concurred entirely with me in opinion
that this was a snare deliberately spread by
Crawford to accomplish the utter ruin of Calhoun." The opportunities for these two men
to be well informed were too good not to require that the greatest weight be accorded to
their opinion. Besides, the powder for the
petard was confessedly furnished by Crawford's guilty indiscretion. He divulged the
secrets of certain of the Cabinet meetings of
Monroe's administration, which filled Jackson's
mind with deep hatred and contempt against
Calhoun. If we were writing the biography of
Andrew Jackson, it would be necessary, in this
connection, to review the whole controversy
concerning the general's conduct in the Semi-
nole war. But in a life of Calhoun we can
with propriety dispense with that thankless
task, confining our remarks to a single point in
it, and even that may be treated with great
brevity.

In the course of his operations against the
Seminoles, General Jackson had not only crossed
the Florida boundary, as he was authorized to
do in case the object of the campaign could not
otherwise be attained, but he had forcibly taken
possession of the Spanish forts at St. Mark's
and Pensacola. In July, 1818, the question as

to whether and how far these high-handed proceedings should be sustained by the administration formed the subject of long and earnest
discussions by Mr. Monroe and his Cabinet.
The general had acted in good faith. A letter
to the President, in which he communicated his
intentions, having accidentally remained unanswered, he mistook the silence for tacit consent,
and afterwards, without regard to dates, even
adduced a subsequent letter of the Secretary of
War to a third person as proof that the government had given him full discretion. This was
by no means the view which Mr. Monroe and
his Cabinet took of the matter. Even Adams,
who went farthest in supporting the general's
course, did not undertake to justify it wholly by
rules of international law, but deemed it necessary to adduce considerations of high policy for
his opinion. Calhoun, as Adams states in his
Diary, " principally bore the argument against
me, insisting that the capture of Pensacola was
not necessary upon principles of self-defence,
and therefore was both an act of war against
Spain and a violation of the Constitution ; that
the administration, by approving it, would take
all the blame of it upon themselves; that by
leaving it upon his responsibility they would
take away from Spain all pretext for war and
for resorting to the aid of other European pow-

ers, — they would also be free from all reproach of having violated the Constitution, — that it was not the menace of the Governor of Pensacola that had determined Jackson to take that place; that he had really resolved to take it before; that he had violated his orders, and upon his own arbitrary will set all authority at defiance." He therefore demanded an investigation of the general's conduct; but although "all the members of the Cabinet, except myself [Adams] are of opinion that Jackson acted not only without, but against, his instructions," and "that he has committed war upon Spain," a middle course was finally adopted, which, without directly and formally disavowing the general, satisfied Spain.

Jackson knew that his conduct had not met with the approval of the administration, but he had heretofore believed that the contemplated proceedings against him had been principally urged by Crawford, and that, on the other hand, Calhoun had exerted himself in his defence. Now, however, a letter from Crawford to Senator Forsyth (April 30, 1830), which had been written for this purpose, was put into his hands, and undeceived him on the latter point, at the same time giving a false and malicious coloring to the whole transaction. If any member of the administration had been animated by a really *hostile* spirit against the general, it had been Crawford; yet Crawford now pretended that, upon learning all the attending circumstances, he had become satisfied that Jackson was fully excused, if not justified. And the weight which he thus shook from his own shoulders he shifted upon the back of Calhoun, by the bold exaggeration that the latter had persistently demanded the *punishment* of the general.

These revelations threw Jackson into a towering passion. On May 13 he sent Crawford's letter with a curt note to Calhoun, demanding " to learn of you whether it be possible that the information given is correct." Calhoun might have declined to answer the interrogatory, because nobody had a right to demand from him a confession concerning what had passed in the Cabinet meetings of the administration, of which he had been a member. He, however, replied with a long statement and elaborate argument, which had too much the character of a justification of his conduct and of an impeachment of Crawford's behavior and motives. Though he proved that Jackson could and ought to have known that the proceedings in Florida were, at the time, considered by him (Calhoun) transgressions of the orders issued from his department, and that he had, without any personal hostility, acted according to his convictions of duty, for which he owed no account to the general either then or now, all such arguments did not avail him anything, and his dignity would have been better served by taking higher ground. Most truly did he say, " It was an affair of mere official duty, involving no question of private enmity or friendship ; " but that was a view which Andrew Jackson was absolutely unable to understand. In theory he may have admitted the possibility of an honest difference of opinion, but whatever related to himself he could only see in an eminently personal light; and if any one whom he deemed his friend had the misfortune and audacity to differ with him, the brand of Cain was indelibly stamped on that man's forehead. All Calhoun got for his pains was violent, impudent, and absurd abuse, mingled with ludicrous pathos. He was charged with " secretly endeavoring to destroy my reputation," while the poor victim " had too exalted an opinion of your honor and frankness to believe for one moment that you could be capable of such deception. . . . I repeat, I had a right to believe that you were my sincere friend, and, until now, never expected to have occasion to say of you, in the language of Cæsar, *Et tu, Brute !* "

The reproach of a lack of frankness was,

however, not quite unfounded, but it was *now*, rather than heretofore, that Calhoun was guilty of it. He declared in his reply of May 29, " I neither questioned your patriotism nor your motives." Adams's Diary, that invaluable source of historical information, furnishes the proof that this was not strictly true. On July 14, 1818, Adams gives it as his impression that " Calhoun, the Secretary of War, generally of sound, judicious, and comprehensive mind, seems in this case to be personally offended with the idea that Jackson has set at naught the instructions of the department." Again, in a short synopsis of a conversation between himself and Calhoun, on March 2, 1831, two weeks after the publication of the correspondence with Jackson, Adams writes, —

" He said, too, that his remark in the Cabinet meeting, in reply to my argument that Jackson's taking the Spanish forts had been defensive, to meet the threats of Masot, namely, that Jackson had determined to take the province before, was not with allusion to the letter of January 6, 1818,[1] but to a rumor that Jackson had been personally interested in a previous land speculation in Pensacola."

This breach with Jackson was the death-blow to the presidential aspirations of Calhoun.

[1] Jackson's letter to the President, before alluded to, which had accidentally remained unanswered.

Mr. Wirt thought "that he had blasted his prospects of future advancement forever," and Adams called him "a drowning man," at the same time, however, asserting that he "nevertheless entertains very sanguine hopes." Perhaps this expression was a little too strong, but at all events Calhoun maintained his candidacy a while longer, although he not only had to encounter the enmity of Jackson's partisans, but could also no longer count upon the support of New England, which had become ill-disposed towards him by reason of the political course of his friends in Congress. It was rumored that Clay's Western friends were inclined to take him up, in case they should find the chances of their own champion desperate, and Calhoun himself seems to have thought it possible that, if he should conclude to run against Jackson, the election might revert once more to the House of Representatives. But the drift of public opinion was too strong not to destroy these illusions very speedily. Calhoun's disappointment was, undoubtedly, very bitter; but those strangely misjudged the man who attributed to it the terrible energy with which he henceforth pursued the course upon which he had entered with the South Carolina Exposition. He was not driven by disappointed ambition into a sectional policy with a view to-

wards tearing the Union asunder, in order to
become the chief of one half, because he could
not be the chief of the whole. Slavery *had*
split the Union into two geographical sections,
and, in spite of everything man could do, the
rent widened into a chasm, and the chasm into
an abyss. That was not the work of Calhoun,
but the unavoidable consequence of the fact
that the Union was composed of free and slave-
holding States. He could not have done it if
he had wanted to, and he was as far as any man
from wanting to do it. The only effect of the
disappointment of his ambition was the quick
dispersion of the mist which had hitherto been
lying over his eyes as over those of the whole
people. The shackles of minor considerations
and personal interests began to fall from his
limbs. Embittered but free, he henceforth pursued his course, forming alliances without heeding the claims of old or new party connections,
and not afraid to encounter the enmity of any
one ; never ceasing to love and cherish the
Union, but learning to love slavery better and
better. He was not a demi-god, but a man,
having his full share of human weakness and
littleness. But nature had not only endowed
him with a powerful brain ; the marrow of his
bones and the core of his heart were sound.
Not for the world would he have betrayed his

country, and even slavery could not turn him into a dark conspirator. Yet it has been pretended that he was guilty of such betrayal and conspiracy merely in order to see the title President prefixed to his name. Those who, like Senator Benton, honestly believed this, stumbled into an egregious blunder, because, in spite of all their keen-sightedness, they remained blind to the fact that the wedlock between slavery and freedom could not be a lasting one. What they attributed to the traitorous machinations of his disappointed ambition would have happened, even though out of every fibre of John C. Calhoun a Henry Clay, a Daniel Webster, and a Thomas Benton had been made. It was not a crime, but it was his misfortune, that he saw everything relating to slavery with such appalling clearness, discerning, with unerring eye, the last consequences at the first glance.

As soon as all hope had to be given up that the protective system could be destroyed with Jackson's help in the regular parliamentary way, Calhoun resumed the contest at the point where he had left it with the South Carolina Exposition. His second manifesto — " Address to the People of South Carolina," dated Fort Hill, July 26, 1831 — was published in the " Pendleton Messenger." The whole question of the relation which the States and the general government bear to each other, *i. e.*, of state sovereignty, was reargued. The key-note of his whole argument and of his whole subsequent political life is the assertion, " The great dissimilarity and, as I must add, as truth compels me to do, contrariety of interests in our country . . . are so great that they cannot be subjected to the unchecked will of a majority of the whole without defeating the great end of government, without which it is a curse, — justice." This is the real broad foundation of his doctrine that the Union could never have a safe foundation upon any other legal basis save state sovereignty, which enables the minority to defend themselves against usurpations. No new argument is adduced either on the constitutional or on the economical question, but the whole reasoning is closer and the language is more direct and bolder. The Federal government has dwindled down to a mere " agent " of the " sovereign States," and the veto power of these is termed " nullification."

Calhoun had, of course, not expected to convince his adversaries. What he wanted was to mark off the old, widely trodden road with the utmost precision, so that in future no gap could be reasoned into it, and to consolidate his own party, and to inspire it with resolution to live up to its profession of faith. The apprehen-

sion that this would be done was great enough
to dampen the ardor of the protectionists when
the tariff question came again before Congress.
The duties were considerably reduced, but the
plantation States were not satisfied either with
the amount or with the manner in which the
reduction was effected. South Carolina received the new tariff as a declaration that the
protective system was "the settled policy of
the country," and on August 28, 1832, Calhoun
issued his third manifesto, determined to have
the die cast without further delay. This letter
to Governor Hamilton, of South Carolina, is the
final and classical exposition of the theory of
state sovereignty. Nothing new has ever been
added to it. All the later discussions of it
have but varied the expressions and amplified
the argument on particular points. Thirty
years later the programme laid down in it was
carried out by the South piece by piece, and
the justification of the Southern course was
based, point by point, upon this argument.

The late champion of a *national* policy and
of *consolidating* measures now takes for his
starting-point the assertion that, "so far from
the Constitution being the work of the American
people collectively, no such political body, either
now or ever, did exist." The historical review
by which he tried to prove this assertion con-

tains two seemingly slight, but in fact very
important, errors. The colonies did not "by
name and enumeration" declare themselves free
and independent States, nor is the Constitution
declared "to be *binding* between the States so
ratifying," but Article VII. of the Constitution
reads, "The ratification of the conventions of
nine States shall be sufficient for the *establishment* of this Constitution between the States so
ratifying." From these historic "facts" he
draws the conclusion "that there is no direct
and immediate connection between the individual
citizens of a State and the general government."
Strange indeed! for the authors and the advocates
of the Constitution thought that the most important change effected in the political structure
of the Union, by substituting the Constitution
for the Articles of Confederation, was exactly
the establishment of direct and immediate connections between the individual citizens and the
Federal government; and not a single day passed
in which a great number of citizens were not
actually brought into contact with the Federal
government, in the courts, in the custom-houses,
in the departments, etc., without being reminded
in any way whatever that they were citizens of
this or that particular State. If the relation
between the individual citizen and the Federal
government were, in fact, exclusively through the

State, then, indeed, it might have been true that "it belongs to the State as a member of the Union, in her sovereign capacity in convention, to determine definitely, as far as her citizens are concerned, the extent of the obligation which she has contracted; and if, in her opinion, the act exercising the power [in dispute] be unconstitutional, to declare it null and void, which declaration would be obligatory on her citizens." The Federal government is floating in the air without a straw of its own to rest upon, the sport of the sovereign fancies of the States. "Not a provision can be found in the Constitution authorizing the general government to exercise any control whatever over a State by force, by veto, by judicial process, or in any other form, — a most important omission, designed, and not accidental." And the actual state of the case corresponds with the right, for "it would be impossible for the general government, within the limits of the States, to execute, legally, the act nullified, while, on the other hand, the State would be able to enforce, legally and peaceably, its declaration of nullification." Yet nullification is declared to be "the great conservative principle" of the Union.

Undoubtedly, there is method in this madness, but madness it is nevertheless; for the whole theory is neither more nor less than the systematization of anarchy. The Union is constructed upon the principle that the essence of the idea *State*, the supremacy of the will which has to act for the whole, — that is, in a free State, the government of the laws, — is by principle excluded from its structure. If there ever was an illustration of the " tragedy of Hamlet with the part of Hamlet left out," here it is. This vast republic, to which the future belonged more than to any other state of the globe, was to be a shooting star, a political monster without a supreme will, because this could be lodged nowhere with safety. The resort to force — "should folly or madness ever make the attempt" — would be utterly vain, if at all possible, for " it would be . . . a conflict of moral, not physical, force." This moral force, however, was also but a rope of sand, if a sovereign State should so will it. Even a decision by three fourths of the States would by no means be unconditionally binding upon all the members of the Union. " Should the other members undertake to grant the power nullified, and should the nature of the power be such as to defeat the object of the association or union, at least as far as the member nullifying is concerned, it would then become an abuse of power on the part of the principals, and thus present a case where secession would apply." The Union was to have laws only so long and just

so far as *every* constituent member of it was
pleased to submit to them. In his great political
testament, the "Disquisition on Government,"
Calhoun directly says, "Nothing short of a
negative, absolute or in effect, on the part of
the government [!] of a State can possibly protect it against the encroachments of the united
government of the States, whenever [!] their
powers come in conflict." And as even this
might prove not to be a sufficient protection,
each State was to have, in the form of the right
of secession, a most absolute veto against all
its co-States. What a nice checker-board the
United States might become, if the exercise of
this right should get to be the political fashion!
Suppose the States at the mouths of the great
streams, and four or five others commanding a
part of their navigable waters, should secede,
what a pretty picture the map of the United
States would present! Why, the German *Bund*
of bygone days would have had a most formidable rival. Calhoun himself would have
turned with disgust and contempt from the idea
of thus bridging over the craggy actualities of
life with the cobwebs of an over-subtle logic, if
he had conceived the possibility of his theory
being ever put into practice in *this* manner. It
seemed to him so plausible *only* because he was
fully conscious of the fact that, if it were ever

put to the test, the Union would split into *two solid geographical sections.* Never would he have stultified his intellect by this ingenious systematization of anarchy, if he could not have written, —

" Who, of any party, with the least pretension to candor, can deny that on all these points [the great questions of trade, of taxation, of disbursement and appropriation, and the nature, character, and power of the general government] so deeply important, no two distinct nations can be more opposed than this [the staple States] and the other sections? "

CHAPTER V

THE SENATE

ON November 24 the South Carolina convention passed the nullification ordinance, which was to take effect on February 1, 1833. Calhoun at once resigned the vice-presidency, in order to take the seat in the United States Senate, vacated by General Hayne, who had been elected Governor of South Carolina. Hundreds of eyes closely scrutinized the face of the "great Nullifier" as he took the oath to support the Constitution, but the firm repose of his countenance dispelled all doubts of his sincerity. His personal courage, however, was seriously questioned by many. Benton and others assure us that he finally yielded, because he had been informed that Jackson had threatened to hang him as high as Haman. This dramatic anecdote has been repeated so often that the mass of the American people have come to believe it as an undoubted historic fact. That Jackson may have uttered some such threat is probable enough, but Calhoun never betrayed such a weakness of nerves as to justify a suspicion that an empty threat could wipe from his brains all remembrance of the Constitution. And an empty threat this most certainly was, if it was ever made. Jackson was not now the general commanding in the wilds of Florida, but President of the United States; and Calhoun was not an Arbuthnot or Ambrister, but a senator of the United States. The section of the Constitution, however, has yet to be written which empowers the President to hang any man, and especially a United States senator. The hanging story may have been good enough at the time for political purposes, but it deserves no place in history. Yet Calhoun knew well enough that not only he personally, but also his State, was playing a high game, in which eventually powder and lead, and perhaps even the hangman, upon the requisition of the courts or of a court-martial, might speak the last word. He therefore did yield, but only because Congress and Jackson — notwithstanding the justly celebrated " proclamation " — yielded still more. The explanations with which Calhoun accompanied his affirmative vote on a certain provision of the tariff bill, after he had declared it unconstitutional, were vain talk; he bent his proud neck, because Mr. Clayton had left him no alternative except to submit, or to let the whole compromise fail. On the other hand, however, the new tariff conceded in the main the demands of South Carolina, and the so-called Force Bill, which gave the President the means to subdue by force of arms any resistance to the laws of the Union, was only passed after the passage of the tariff bill had been fully secured. Congress, with the reluctant approval of the President, bought the acquiescence of South Carolina, and then the daring little State was told that she would have been crushed had she persisted in her mad course. A dread — honorable and patriotic indeed, but on the part of the Federal government much to be regretted — of the consequences had forced both parties from their original standpoint. The principle was purposely left undecided, and, as to the immediate practical questions, a compromise was effected ; but if either party had a right to claim the victory, it was certainly not Jackson and the majority of Congress, but Calhoun and South Carolina.

Another, and perhaps the best, proof that apprehensions for his personal safety, on account of Jackson's reported threats, had nothing to do with the course pursued by Calhoun, is the calmness with which he reviewed the field after the contest was over. There was not a single man in either camp who judged the results of it more correctly than he. Whenever a suitable opportunity was offered, he claimed, in a calm and dignified but very decided manner, that the overthrow of the protective system was due to the resistance offered by South Carolina, and that the conservative and beneficial character of nullification had been proved by experience. At the same time, however, he never failed to acknowledge that the doctrine of states-rights had suffered a defeat by the passage of the Force Bill. He even laid greater stress upon this fact, and exaggerated its significance. On April 9, 1834, he delivered a speech in support of a bill, which he had introduced, to repeal the obnoxious act, although by its own limitation the power conferred by it on the President was to expire at the termination of this session. Those who charged him with doing so only in order to appear consistent greatly deceived themselves. From the moment that he had assumed the leadership of the states-rights party the *principiis obsta* was always present to his mind, and the unswerving rigor with which he applied it goes far to explain why he held such a unique position among the Southern statesmen in the slavery conflict. " The precedent, unless the act be expunged from the statute-book, will live forever, ready, on any pretext of future danger, to be quoted as an authority to confer on the chief magistrate similar or even more dangerous powers, if more dangerous can be devised." Therefore he declared it "subversive of our political institutions, and fatal to the liberty and happiness of the country," although, as to the immediate object for which it purported to be passed, the compromise tariff had rendered it a piece of waste paper ere it had been inscribed on the statute-book. He was not lulled into the sleep of false security by the calm after the first blast of the storm. Already in the so-called Edgefield letter of March 27, 1833, declining an invitation to a public dinner, he had written, "The struggle to preserve the liberty and Constitution of the country, and to arrest the corrupt and dangerous tendency of the government, so far from being over, is not more than fairly commenced. . . . Let us not deceive ourselves by supposing that the danger is past. We have but checked the disease. If one evil has been remedied, another has succeeded."

As he declined all public demonstrations proposed to be given in acknowledgment of the stand he had taken against the Federal government, because he did not want to carry fuel to the fire of his calumniators, who attributed his course solely to impure personal motives, so also he abstained from currying the favor of his own party by shouting triumph and flattering them

with pæans. To sound the tocsin was the un-
grateful task of the rest of his life, and the
greater the success of the slave power the harder
he pulled the rope. In August, 1833, he wrote
to the citizens of Newton County, who had ten-
dered him a public dinner, —

"I utter it under a painful but a solemn conviction
of its truth that we are no longer a free people, — a
people living under a Constitution, as the guardian of
their rights; but under the absolute rule of an unchecked majority, which has usurped the power to do
as it pleases, and to enforce its pleasure at the point
of the bayonet. . . . This condition we had been long
approaching; and to it we are now absolutely reduced by the proclamation and force act. . . . So
long, then, as the act of blood stains our statute-book,
and the sovereignty of the States is practically denied
by the government, so long will be the duration of
our political bondage."

This is the *ceterum censeo*, which recurs in all
his speeches during the next years. In his first
great speech after the nullification session, he
declared, —

"I stand wholly disconnected with the two great
parties now contending for ascendency. My political
connections are with that small and denounced party
which has voluntarily retired from the party strifes
of the day, with a view of saving, if possible, the liberty and the Constitution of the country in this great
crisis of our affairs."

He had not become a Whig, nor had he ceased to be a Democrat, but he was one of the most uncompromising adversaries of Jacksonism. In all the leading questions of these years, so full of bitter strife, he stands in the front rank of the opposition, but he has no more in common with Clay and Webster than before. He and they fought side by side *against* a common enemy, but he did not fight with them *for* a common cause. In their defensive warfare against the removal of the government deposits from the United States Bank, these three occupied the same ground ; but when it came to the question of renewing the charter of the bank, or to the general problem of the currency, their ways separated, though they did not diverge so much as one would suppose from Calhoun's subsequent course.

With regard to the bank, he sat as yet, so to say, on the fence. He did not conceal the lively distrust and grave apprehensions with which he viewed the close connection of the government with a privileged moneyed corporation of such enormous means, but the reasons of expediency still prevailed over the objections which would have been decisive with him, if he had felt free to follow his inclination and general principles. He himself even reminded the Senate of the fact that the bank would

probably not have been established, if it had
not been for his exertions. His argumentation
was as clear and logical as usual, and it led him
to definite practical propositions; and yet his
speeches leave the impression upon the reader's
mind that he himself did not know exactly
what to think and what to will. Like the country, he was in a state of transition with regard
to this perplexing problem, and it is a curious
fact that so early as 1834 he pointed out the
ultimate solution of it; but he did it in such a
way that it would be absurd to claim for him
the honor of the discovery. In his speech of
January 13, on the removal of the deposits, he
said, —

"So long as the question is one between a Bank of
the United States, incorporated by Congress, and that
system of banks which has been created by the will
of the Executive, it is an insult to the understanding
to discourse on the pernicious tendency and unconsti-
tutionality of the Bank of the United States. To
bring up that question fairly and legitimately, you
must go one step farther: you must *divorce* the government and the banking system. You must refuse
all connection with banks. You must neither receive
nor pay away bank-notes; you must go back to the
old system of the strong-box, and of gold and silver.
. . . I repeat, you must *divorce* the government entirely from the banking system; or, if not, you are

bound to incorporate a bank as the only safe and efficient means of giving stability and uniformity to the currency."

Calhoun was not a "statesman" of the type which, at this time, began to become only too common in the United States. He did not owe his position to the grace of King Caucus and the favor of his grandees, the washed and unwashed patriots of the primary meetings. He therefore did not know and understand everything by intuition, as this privileged class of mortals do, but he was obliged to study and reflect upon the subjects with which he had to deal as a legislator. As a seat in the legislative hall was in his opinion as well the most responsible as the most honorable post in which a man can be put by the confidence of his fellow citizens, he applied himself to this task with all the thoroughgoing earnestness of his nature. It is therefore a matter of course that his speeches never lacked a positive element of more or less, and not unfrequently of considerable, merit. Yet ever since the Southern Samson has put his head into the lap of the Delilah of state sovereignty, his strength is on the wane whenever he returns to his old place among the builders of his country's greatness and happiness. Critically to dissect the arguments of others and to expose the weak points of their devices, to de-

nounce their inconsistencies and mercilessly to
lash the moral shortcomings of their policy,
and, above all, to point out the breakers ahead
of the ship of state, — these are the things in
which he excels.

Jackson's administration offered a wide field
for the vigorous application of all these peculiar
qualities, and it was but human that Calhoun
should avail himself the more willingly of the
opportunity on account of his personal relations
with the President. His speeches on the removal of the deposits and on Jackson's protest
against the resolution of the Senate, denouncing
it as an unwarrantable assumption of power, exposed the President's high-handed way of dealing with the Constitution and the laws, also the
gross fallacies and inconsistencies of his reasoning, in a truly masterly way, and were not less
admirable defences of the constitutional rights
and privileges of the legislative branch of the
government. He did not spare the President,
but neither his personal grievances nor the intensity of his political anger and disgust carried
him beyond the line which respect for the office
ought to draw whenever the chief magistrate of
the republic is spoken of; and his most vigorous
thrusts were not aimed against the person, but
against the system which had been inaugurated
by Jackson.

If the high-toned moral severity of the above-mentioned speeches was seasoned now and then with cutting irony and haughty defiance, Calhoun's remarks on the wholesale dismissal of Federal office-holders without cause betray patriotic sadness and deep anxiety for the future of his country. The subject was of too serious a nature to permit him to indulge in personal animosities or party bickerings. The removal of the deposits, the protest, the whole bank question, though all of great import, were after all but questions of the day, which would soon be dead issues, of no interest to anybody except the student of history. But would not the very life-blood of the body politic be poisoned if the government should fall into the hands of mercenaries, with whom politics constituted only a trade, to which they devoted themselves for the sake of the "spoils" of office? Was not the love of country in danger of being drowned in the whirlpools of party strife, if the official spokesmen of the national parties should be men who owed their position to the dexterity with which they gathered followers around their standards by means of the spoils? Would not the politics of the republic degenerate more and more from a contest about great public measures, principles, and ideas, into a mean scuffle about the husks, if it should become an acknowledged

principle that " to the victor belong the spoils " ?
Would not every party be forced to follow suit
if the example should be once successfully set,
— for what party could hope to vanquish with
untrained volunteers the skilled bands of lans-
quenets fighting for booty? Would not the
management of the public affairs rapidly sink
until it became a byword, if, instead of fitness
for the office, the services rendered to the party,
or rather to the chiefs of the party, should become the criterion for all the appointments, and
if the Federal offices should come to be filled
with those who had not succeeded in private
life; for would not the others at best consider
the Federal offices but momentary make-shifts, if
ability and faithfulness could no longer secure
their tenure? Last, but not least, would not the
people begin to turn with disgust from politics
when they saw the statesmen more and more
ousted by mere bread-and-butter politicians?
And what is the life of a democratic republic
worth if the people accustom themselves to consider politics the monopoly of a set of men whom
they do not respect?

In his speech on the removal of the deposits,
Calhoun had said, with burning indignation : —

" Can he [Secretary Taney] be ignorant that the
whole power of the government has been perverted
into a great political machine, with a view of cor-

rupting and controlling the country? Can he be
ignorant that the avowed and open policy of the
government is to reward political friends and punish
political enemies? . . . With money we will get partisans, with partisans votes, and with votes money, is
the maxim of our public pilferers. . . . With money
and corrupt partisans a great effort is now making to
choke and stifle the voice of American liberty through
all its constitutional and legal organs by pensioning
the press; by overawing the other departments; and
finally by setting up a new organ, composed of office-
holders and partisans, under the name of a National
Convention, which, counterfeiting the voice of the
people, will, if not resisted, in their name dictate the
succession."

In a speech of February 13, 1835, he summed
up the ultimate results of the spoils system in
the following words : —

" When it comes to be once understood that politics are a game ; that those who are engaged in it but
act a part ; that they make this or that profession not
from honest conviction or an intent to fulfil them, but
as the means of deluding the people, and through
that delusion to acquire power, — when such profes-
sions are to be entirely forgotten, the people will lose
all confidence in public men ; all will be regarded as
mere jugglers, — the honest and the patriotic as well
as the cunning and the profligate ; and the people will
become indifferent and passive to the grossest abuses
of power on the ground that those whom they may

elevate, under whatever pledges, instead of reforming
will but imitate the example of those whom they
have expelled."

Does not this passage read like a cutting from
an editorial of the last number of an "independent" newspaper of the present day, advocating
civil service reform? But though he foresaw
with astonishing perspicacity what this mis-
chievous innovation must inevitably lead to, the
root of the evil and the remedy for it he discovered no more than did any of his contemporaries. The uniform practice of the preceding
administrations concerning dismissal from office
— even Jefferson's hardly forming an exception,
although the loud complaints of the opposition
had not been wholly unfounded — made him
believe that nothing more was needed than to
deprive the President of the power which, as
he contended, had been conferred upon him
under a mistaken construction of the Constitution. He himself, as he openly avowed, had
formerly held the opposite opinion, and the argument with which he supported the assertion
that the power of appointing did not imply that
of dismissing was more ingenious than profound
and sound. But whatever the true answer to
the constitutional question be, the great mistake
lay in the supposition that the evil could be
cured by putting the power of dismissal from

office under the direct control of Congress or the Senate. Experience has proved that Congress was more to be feared than the President; for, in spite of the clear provision of the Constitution, even the power of appointment has in the main virtually passed from the hands of the President into those of the members of Congress; and the civil service reformers of our days usually consider this the worst feature of the actual system. Calhoun, like the whole Whig opposition, mistook a mere symptom for the cause of the disease. Because Jackson's administration assumed more and more the character of the reign of an autocrat, they apprehended that the encroachments of the Executive upon the domain of the other departments of the government, and more especially the legislative, would continue to undermine the Constitution until the whole fabric of republican liberty should be in danger of toppling to the ground. The above-quoted denunciation of the National Convention, "composed of office-holders and partisans," which was to "dictate the succession," closed with the following words: "When the deed shall have been done, the revolution completed, and all the powers of our republic, in like manner, consolidated in the Executive and perpetuated by his dictation." Calhoun and the Whigs failed to see that, who-

soever might become President, it could not
possibly be an Andrew Jackson II. Jackson
might be powerful enough virtually to nomi-
nate his *successor*, but to appoint an *heir* was
beyond his power. The presidential office was
only the means of exercising this extraordinary
power; but the source of it was the peculiar
disposition of the majority of the people towards
him, and this peculiar disposition was a thing
which he could not bequeath to anybody. Van
Buren knew this so well that in his letter accept-
ing the nomination by the Baltimore Convention he humbly declared, " As well from inclination as from duty, I shall, if honored with
the choice of the American people, endeavor to
tread generally in the footsteps of President
Jackson." He was Jackson's choice, but the
heirs of the general were the politicians, and
Van Buren would never have occupied the
White House if he had not been one of the
master minds of the politicians. If he had ever
presumed to speak in Jackson's tone and to act
in his autocratic spirit, the " Sage of Kinder-
hook " would have been considered by his own
party to be out of his senses.

March 4, 1837, did not inaugurate a second
" era of good feeling." The opposition remained loud and passionate, but the melodies
of their war-songs were changed, or they were

at least sung in another key. To pretend that
Martin Van Buren would " name " his successor,
and that there was still immediate danger of
the liberties of the country being crushed by
the consolidation of all powers in the Executive,
would have been simply ridiculous. The fears
entertained on this head during the administration of Jackson had certainly not been fictitious,
though they had been generally very highly
colored for the sake of effect. The best proof
of their serious character was furnished by a
movement for an amendment to the Constitution, abolishing the veto power of the President.
Calhoun, however, had not so far lost the sobriety of his judgment as to approve of this idea.
He declared the veto " indispensable," because
without it " the independence of the President,"
so far as concerned Congress, would be destroyed.
He shared for the moment the erroneous views
of the Whigs as to the future, but as to the
past, *i. e.*, the origin of the evil, he went farther
back than they. The encroachments of the
Executive upon the legislative and judicial
department of the government were with him
" the *second* stage of the revolution ; " but it
had begun " many years ago, with the commencement of the restrictive system, and terminated its first stage with the passage of the
Force Bill of the last session, which absorbed

all the rights and sovereignty of the States, and consolidated them in this government." Thus his argument returned to its starting-point. The only way to secure "the preservation of our institutions" was to adopt the doctrine of state sovereignty with all its consequences; and the last cause of all the evils complained of, by which the liberty of the country, and perhaps even the existence of the republic, were put in jeopardy, was the violation of this fundamental principle by the Federal government.

From this time forward, every speech of Calhoun which is not strictly confined to some special subject, contains a repetition of these two assertions in some form or other, and his inclination is constantly growing to make the range for his observations, on all subjects whatsoever, wide enough to permit some remarks on these topics, or at least a passing allusion to them. The wiseacres, who laughed all the warnings of the alarmists to scorn, began to consider him a kind of monomaniac on this head. Yet it was they whose minds wandered through the dales and o'er the hills of cloud-land, while his feet remained firmly planted on the rock of actualities. Every day the slavery question became more exclusively the needle which determined the course of the politics of the country, and if safety for the interests of the slave-holders

could be obtained at all in the Union, it was
only through the doctrine of state sovereignty.
No one understood so well as Calhoun that the
appearance of the abolitionists had laid the axe
to the root of slavery, though they were but a
handful of men and women, with neither fame,
social position, office, money, nor the general
approbation of the public mind to make them
formidable adversaries ; and therefore as yet no
one fully understood how terribly in earnest
he was and how correctly he read the future,
when he declared at every opportunity that the
minority, that is the South, was doomed, if state
sovereignty was not recognized as the central
pillar on which the dome of the Constitution
rested.

In January, 1831, William Lloyd Garrison
had established in Boston " The Liberator," with
the programme of " immediate and unconditional
emancipation," and in December, 1833, the
American Anti-Slavery Society had put forth
its " declaration of principles," declaring against
slavery a war which excluded the possibility
of peace. The slave States were thrown into
a wild excitement by the proceedings of the
enthusiastic little band, and in the North the
mob, very generally countenanced by public
opinion and even by the authorities, had begun
to hunt the agitators down as criminals who,

like Western horse-thieves, were of too dangerous a character to be admitted within the pale
of the law. Some time, however, was yet to
elapse ere the question came directly before
Congress. An occasional remark on " the fanatics and madmen of the North, who are waging
war against the domestic institutions of the
South, under the plea of promoting the general
welfare," is therefore about all we hear from
Calhoun on this subject, during the first years.
But when at last the discussion made its way
into the halls of legislation he at once took part
in it in a manner which proved that for a long
time all his faculties had been concentrated
upon the topic; for he, and he alone, fully mastered it.

CHAPTER VI

SLAVERY

In the Senate the floodgates of debate were opened by Calhoun's motion (January 7, 1836) not to receive two petitions for the abolition of slavery in the District of Columbia. The war of words, in which nearly one half of all the senators took part, lasted until March 11. Even by his Southern colleagues Calhoun was severely reproved for opening this box of Pandora. They accused him of going on a quixotic expedition in search of abstract political principles, because he himself declared that the abolitionists could not possibly "entertain the slightest hope that Congress would pass a law, at this time, to abolish slavery in this District, . . . and that seriously to attempt it would be fatal to their cause." Was it not a frivolous playing with fire and powder to force the discussion of this question upon Congress, since the material rights and interests of the South were absolutely secured by the perfect unanimity of Congress, most energetically backed by public opinion in all the Northern States? Would not this

uncalled-for debate do more to promote the
cause of abolitionism than all the pamphlets
and emissaries of the abolitionists had been
able to do? For whether his constitutional
argument was sound or not, it was an incontestable fact that his motion was considered by
the North a wanton attack upon the right of
petition.

There was undoubtedly a good deal of truth
in all these objections to the course pursued by
Calhoun. Yet the charge was wholly unfounded
that he was endeavoring intentionally to in-
cense the North and the South against each
other, in order to promote the purposes of his
party. He spoke the simple truth when he
asserted, in his speech of March 9, 1836, that,
"however calumniated and slandered," he had
"ever been devotedly attached" to the Union
and the institutions of the country, and that he
was "anxious to perpetuate them to the latest
generation." He acted under the firm conviction of an imperious duty towards the South
and towards the Union, and his assertion was
but too well founded that these petitions for the
abolition of slavery in the District of Columbia
were blows on the wedge, which would ultimately break the Union asunder.

That the attack of the abolition petitions was
not directed against slavery in the States, but

merely against slavery in the District, was, though not from the legal point of view, yet as to the ultimate practical result, matter of absolute indifference. If, as all the petitions asserted, the nature of slavery made its existence in the District a national disgrace and a national sin, the same disgrace and the same sin weighed down every Southern State. Calhoun's assertion, therefore, could not be refuted, that "the petitions were in themselves a foul slander on nearly one half of the States of the Union." If the national legislature now, in any way, offered its assistance to brand the peculiar institution of one half of the constituent members of the Union, it certainly violated the spirit of the Constitution; for the Constitution, as everybody admitted, not only tacitly recognized slavery as a fact which the States exclusively had power to deal with, but moreover served in many essential respects as its direct support and protection. Calhoun was therefore unquestionably right when he said that, unless an undoubted provision of the Constitution compelled them to receive such petitions, it was their duty to reject them at the very threshold; and he proved that there was no such absolute compulsion by an undoubted constitutional provision. On the other hand, however, inasmuch as some obligations were imposed upon the whole Union with regard to slavery, the existence of slavery in some of the States was actually and legally also a concern of those States in which it did not exist. And in respect to whatever actually and legally concerned the people, they had a constitutional right to demand that their representatives should listen to their wishes and grievances presented in the form of petitions. Besides, no ingenuity could reason out of the Constitution the power of Congress over slavery in the District; for somewhere the power had to be lodged, and the legislative power of Congress over the District was expressly declared to be "*exclusive* in all cases whatsoever." To lay down the principle that Congress was in duty bound to shut its door against all anti-slavery petitions was therefore most certainly an abridgment of the right of petition. The opponents of Calhoun were, in fact, no less right than he. Not their arguments, but the facts, and the Constitution, which had been framed according to the facts, were at fault. The founders of the republic had been under the necessity of admitting slavery into the Constitution, and the inevitable consequence was that conclusions which were diametrically opposed to each other could be logically deduced from it by starting the argument *first* from the fact that slavery was an acknowledged and protected institution, which, so far as the States were concerned, was out of the pale of the Federal jurisdiction ; and *then* from the no less incontestable fact that the determining principle of the Constitution was liberty, and that the spirit and the whole life of the American people fully accorded with the Constitution in this respect.

The flaw in all the reasoning of Calhoun on the slavery question was, that he took no account whatever of the latter fact. The logical consequence of this was that his constitutional theories were of a nature which rendered the acquiescence of the North in them an utter impossibility. He never became fully conscious of this fact, which rendered all his exertions to obtain absolute safety for slavery *in the Union* as vain as the pouring of water into a cask without a bottom. His reasoning on the dangers which threatened slavery in the actual Union, under the actual Constitution, was, however, not in the least affected by it. From the first he saw them with such an appalling clearness that his predictions could not but seem hallucinations of a diseased mind so long as the people, both at the North and at the South, had not been taught by bitter experience that the conflict was irrepressible, because a compromise between antagonistic principles is *ab initio* an impossibility. From the first he saw, predicted,

and proved that, unless his constitutional doctrines were accepted, slavery could not be safe
in the Union, and that therefore the slave States
would have to cut the ties which bound them
to the North.

"Our true position [he declared in the above-
mentioned speech], that which is indispensable to
our defence *here*, is that Congress has no legitimate
jurisdiction over the subject of slavery either here or
elsewhere. The reception of this petition surrenders
this commanding position ; yields the question of jurisdiction, so important to the cause of abolition and
so injurious to us ; compels us to sit in silence to witness the assault on our character and institutions, or
to engage in an endless contest in their defence. Such
a contest is beyond mortal endurance. We must in
the end be humbled, degraded, broken down, and
worn out.

"The senators from the slave-holding States, who,
most unfortunately, have committed themselves to
vote for receiving these incendiary petitions, tell us
that whenever the attempt shall be made to abolish
slavery they will join with us to repel it. . . . But I
announce to them that they are now called on to re-
deem their pledge. *The attempt is* now *being made.*
The work is going on daily and hourly. The war is
waged not only in the most dangerous manner, but
in the only manner that it can be waged. Do they
expect that the abolitionists will resort to arms, and
commence a crusade to liberate our slaves by force ?

Is this what they mean when they speak of the attempt to abolish slavery? If so, let me tell our friends of the South who differ from us that the war which the abolitionists wage against us is of a very different character, and far more effective. It is a war of religious and political fanaticism, mingled, on the part of the leaders, with ambition and the love of notoriety, and waged not against our lives, but our character. The object is to humble and debase us in our own estimation, and that of the world in general; to blast our reputation, while they overthrow our domestic institutions. This is the mode in which they are attempting abolition, with such ample means and untiring industry; and *now is the time* for all who are opposed to them to meet the attack. How can it be successfully met? This is the important question. There is but one way: we must meet the enemy on the frontier, — on the question of receiving; we must secure that important pass, — it is our Thermopylæ. The power of resistance, by an universal law of nature, is on the exterior. Break through the shell, penetrate the crust, and there is no resistance within. In the present contest, the question on receiving constitutes our frontier. It is the first, the exterior question, that covers and protects all others. Let it be penetrated by receiving this petition, and not a point of resistance can be found within, as far as this government is concerned. If we cannot maintain ourselves there, we cannot on any interior position. . . . There is no middle ground that is tenable."

Has not the history of the slavery conflict
fully borne out every one of these assertions?
Calhoun reads the future as if the book of fate
were lying wide open before him. Only as to
the means by which he proposed to avert the
impending dangers he was as blind as all the
rest of the people. If the enlistment of the
moral and religious sentiment of the world
against slavery was a war, in which the South
must ultimately break down, what was the use
of hermetically closing the Capitol at Washington against all the manifestations of the spirit
of abolitionism? Since when did the civilized
world or even the American people wait for
the gracious permission of Congress, ere they
dared to form their religious opinions or moral
convictions? And if the religious, moral, and
political convictions of Congress and of the
people did not agree, which of the two would
finally have to yield, Congress or the people?
Even if it had been but a political question,
the attempt would have been simply absurd
to decree it out of existence by a resolution
of the legislature not to listen to what the people had to say about it. But if it was also
a moral and religious question — which most
certainly it was — the attempt was doubly absurd. There is no " frontier " which can be
successfully defended against ideas, and no

" shell " is so hard that such ideas cannot penetrate it. The confession that, if the shell were
broken through, there was no resistance within,
amounted therefore to a confession that slavery
would at last succumb, if the slave-holding
States remained in the Union.

From all sides Calhoun was accused of stir-
ring up sectional animosity and strife in a most
unwarrantable manner, by exciting the South
with his wild talk about awful dangers, which
had nowhere any existence except in his own
feverish brain. The truth, however, was that
he did not see spectres in broad daylight, but
that he took too hopeful a view of the future.
What in his opinion was but a dire eventuality,
which could be easily averted, was, by his own
showing, the inevitable end of the slavery conflict. Abolitionism tolled the death-bell of slavery *in the Union*, and dearly have the American people had to pay for it, that they ever
doubted Calhoun's declaration that, whenever
the slave-holding States had to choose between
the Union and slavery, they would not hesitate
for a moment to decide in favor of slavery.

" We love and cherish the Union ; we remember
with the kindest feelings our common origin, with
pride our common achievements, and fondly anticipate the common greatness and glory that seem to
await us : but origin, achievements, and anticipation

of common greatness are to us as nothing, compared with this question. It is to us a vital question. It involves not only our liberty, but, what is greater (if to freemen anything can be), existence itself. The relation which now exists between the two races in the slave-holding States has existed for two centuries. It has grown with our growth, and strengthened with our strength. It has entered into and modified all our institutions, civil and political. None other can be substituted. We will not, cannot, permit it to be destroyed. . . . Come what will, should it cost every drop of blood and every cent of property, we must defend ourselves ; and if compelled, we would stand justified by all laws, human and divine ; . . . we would act under an imperious necessity. There would be to us but one alternative, — to triumph or perish as a people. . . . I ask neither sympathy nor compassion for the slave-holding States. We can take care of ourselves. It is not we, but the Union, which is in danger. . . . We cannot remain here in an endless struggle in defence of our character, our property and institutions."

Calhoun spoke to deaf ears. The petition was received, but the prayer of the petitioners was rejected by an overwhelming majority after a short and unimportant debate, in which the South was repeatedly and emphatically assured that thus a precedent was to be established for the rejection of all similar petitions, without any discussion, directly after their reception.

James Buchanan was the father of the great
device of thus, with an obliging compliment to
both sides, slipping through between the hammer and the anvil. It was a new trial of the old
art of cloaking by empty formulas the contradiction of principles and the collision of facts. The
petitioners did not see any material difference
between a refusal to receive and a rejection on
principle without any discussion; and the principle, on the unconditional maintenance of which
alone, in Calhoun's opinion, the safety of slavery depended, was surrendered. Ill-will against
the South had nothing whatever to do with
that. Though slavery was not liked in the
Northern States, they were as yet but too willing to satisfy the demands of the South. They
shunned the agitation of the slavery question
more than did the South, and they were most
willing to suppress abolitionism. The trouble
only was that there was no way of doing it.
It is hardly to be supposed that the more intelligent and educated Southerners can have
deemed it possible for the North to adopt the
means which the Southern radicals proposed,
with insulting imperiousness; and yet there was
a goodly number of Northern politicians who
readily consented to decree even the impossible.

President Jackson's message of December 2,
1835, had invited Congress to pass a law pro-

hibiting, " under severe penalties, the circulation in the Southern States, through the mail,
of incendiary publications intended to instigate
slaves to insurrection." In point of fact, no
such publication had ever been issued by any
American press; but what the President really
wanted was, of course, clear enough: the mails
should be closed to all publications tainted with
the spirit of abolitionism. On Calhoun's motion, this part of the message was referred to a
special committee, which, on February 4, 1836,
introduced a bill, accompanied by a report.
Calhoun, who was the author of the bill and of
the report, defended them on April 12, 1836,
in one of the most remarkable speeches ever
delivered either by him or by anybody else in
Congress. The recommendation of the President was rejected, because a law " discrimi-
nating, in reference to character, what publications shall not be transmitted by the mail,"
would be an abridgment of the liberty of the
press. Moreover, and above all, the principle
upon which such a law would have rested delivered the South, bound hand and foot, to the
discretion of the Federal government. If Congress had the right to determine what publications were incendiary and to forbid their transmission through the mail, it evidently had also
the right to decide what publications were not

incendiary and to enforce their transmission through the mail. Both objections were unquestionably well founded, and an unsophisticated mind would have naturally expected to see the conclusion drawn from them that the publications of the abolitionists could not be legally excluded from the mail. The bill, however, prohibited "deputy-postmasters from receiving and transmitting through the mail, to any State, Territory, or District, certain papers therein mentioned, the circulation of which is prohibited by the laws of said State, Territory, or District." Calhoun, in fact, demanded at least as emphatically as Jackson the exclusion of abolition publications from the mail, and even the means by which he proposed to attain his end were virtually the same, though they appeared under a different nomenclature. The only real difference between the President and the senator was the constitutional doctrine on which they based their respective demands; but that was indeed a difference of the last importance. Jackson's idea was simply that, as slavery was an institution recognized by the Constitution, the Federal government could not allow itself to be used for undermining it, but was obliged to protect it against attacks which were not only "unconstitutional," but "repugnant to the principles of our national compact

and to the dictates of humanity and religion."
Calhoun, on the other hand, took exactly the
opposite view. According to him, the Federal
government had no right to meddle in any way
whatever with this question; all it could do,
and what at the same time was bound to do, was
to enjoin upon its officers to conform themselves
strictly to the laws of the State in which they
happened to be employed.

"The internal peace and security of the States
are under the protection of the States themselves, to
the entire exclusion of all authority and control on
the part of Congress. It belongs to them, and not
to Congress, to determine what is or is not calculated
to disturb their peace and security. . . . In the
execution of the measures which may be adopted by
the States for this purpose [to prohibit the circulation
of any publication or any intercourse calculated to
disturb or destroy the relation between master and
slave], the powers of Congress over the mail, and of
regulating commerce with foreign nations and between
the States, may require coöperation on the part of the
general government; and it is bound, in conformity
with the principle established, to respect the laws of
the State in their exercise, and so to modify its acts
as not only not to violate those of the States, but, as
far as practicable, to coöperate in their execution."

Calhoun's bill, therefore, provided that postmasters who "knowingly" transmitted or delivered any "paper" treating of slavery in a

way contrary to the laws of the State should
be punished by fine and imprisonment. Which
clause of the Constitution conferred upon Congress the power to enact national laws for fur-
thering the execution of the state laws, this
strictest of the strict constructionists forgot to
tell. Like a noble steed on the race-course he
did not look to the right nor to the left, his
course leading in a straight line to the goal. If
he had but once cast a passing glance on either
side, he could hardly have helped being himself
amused at the strange consequences of his theory, if nature had not denied him all sense of
humor so far as politics were concerned. The
laws of the States on the incriminated publications might be as different as the glass splinters
and the little pebbles in a kaleidoscope vary in
shape and color. The Federal law, therefore,
would enjoin upon the postmasters to obey and
execute some dozen different and perhaps even
contradictory laws relating to the same subject,
— a law which would at all events have the
merit of novelty in the history of legislation.
A postmaster in Massachusetts imprisoned for
omitting to do a certain thing, and a postmaster in South Carolina imprisoned for doing this
very thing, both punished in pursuance of the
same Federal law, — these two gentlemen, if no
one else, would certainly not be convinced of
the soundness of Calhoun's theory.

The United States statutes were not disfig-
ured by such a monstrous law. The blot is
sufficiently ugly that it received in the Senate
nineteen votes, four of which were cast by Northern senators. Calhoun himself had probably not
expected a more favorable result, for even of the
four Southern members of the committee only
Mangum, of North Carolina, besides himself,
had given the report and the bill an unqualified
approval. The whole speech of April 12, 1836,
gives the impression that its real purpose was
not so much to convince the Senate of the necessity or propriety of passing this particular bill
as to get the argument before the country as a
new manifesto, or rather *pronunciamento*, of the
slave power. At all events, it is only from this
point of view that it is of great importance.

Calhoun had taken a great step beyond the
standpoint which he had occupied during the
nullification controversy. Then he had said
that the Federal government and the States
were parties to a compact having no common
judge, and therefore each was entitled to decide
for itself as to the extent of its obligations
under the compact, as to the violations of the
same by the other party, and as to the means
and the measure of the remedy. Only at this
subsequent stage, and in evident contradiction
of the alleged "party" relation, was the national

government made to assume the position of an
" agent" of the States. Now we hear nothing
more of a compact; the Federal government
stands no more on an equal footing with the
States; it appears only in the character of their
agent, and a most humble, nay, a pitiful and
despicable agent it is, for it is bound to do the
bidding of every one of its constituent members,
no matter how contradictory, how absurd, how
outrageous their behests may be. Yet Calhoun
has not changed his general constitutional theory
concerning the relation between the Federal
government and the States. It appears in a
modified light only because he does not confine
his reasoning to the constitutional question.
The history of the slavery question has forced
him boldly to step beyond it, and plant his foot
on the higher and firmer ground of the unalterable facts. He holds fast to the Constitution,
for he shares the almost idolatrous veneration of
the whole people for it; he knows how to find
in it what he needs, and he is fully conscious that
he would be a general without a single soldier
in his army from the moment when his theories
and his practical demands should avowedly
come into conflict with its provisions. But the
leading idea of his whole argument is the too
well-founded conviction that, whether in conformity with the Constitution or not, the issue

would be decided according to the facts. Slavery is, in his opinion, not only a fact, but an immutable fact, because it is the direct outgrowth of the natural relation between the white and the black races.

" To destroy the existing relations would be to destroy this prosperity [of the Southern States], and to place the two races in a state of conflict, which must end in the expulsion or extirpation of one or the other. No other can be substituted compatible with their peace or security. The difficulty is in the diversity of the races. So strongly drawn is the line between the two in consequence, and so strengthened by the force of habit and education, that it is impossible for them to exist together in the community, where their numbers are so nearly equal as in the slave-holding States, under any other relation than that which now exists. Social and political equality between them is impossible. No power on earth can overcome the difficulty. The causes lie too deep in the principles of our nature to be surmounted. But, without such equality, to change the present condition of the African race, were it possible, would be but to change the form of slavery."

When the Republicans, many years later, made the political and social equality of the freedmen one of the principal planks of their party platform, they never, to the knowledge of the author, quoted this declaration of Calhoun, though a higher authority than the foremost representative of the slave-holders could, of course, not be adduced for the necessity of such a radical change in the relation of the two races. This is the best proof that, although, or perhaps precisely *because*, Calhoun was the fanatical champion of the ideas of the Middle Ages with regard to *slavery*, he was so far in advance of his times with regard to the *slavery question*, that his prophetic warnings could not possibly be of any use to the country. They were always attentively listened to, here with patriotic anger, there with scorn and disdain, and by some with an involuntary shudder; but nobody really brought them home to his understanding, and therefore they were too soon forgotten, to be transmitted as a portentous bequest to the generation which was to work out their fulfilment in wading through an ocean of blood. Many suspected him of treason, while he performed only with a sorrowing heart the office of a Cassandra; they accused him of planning the destruction of the Union, while he heaped one irrefutable argument upon another, proving the impossibility of the maintenance of slavery in the Union; and when the very "dough-faces" began to see that their clamoring for peace was as the whistling of a boy against the storm, they charged him with being the principal author of

the catastrophe, because he had foretold it.
His claim to a place among the first men who
have acted a part on the political stage of the
United States has never been contested, and yet
he has been handed down to posterity a mere
distorted shadow of the real man, because his
incessant cries of "Beware!" and "Woe to
you!" remained fresh in the memory of the
people, while the reasoning of which these warnings had been but the last conclusion was forgotten or misconstrued.   Yet in spite of all this,
he and those to whom his memory has been
dear have had no right to complain, because,
though he was no traitor, but honestly and earnestly wished to see the Union preserved, still
the Union and all that made it valuable and
dear to him were " *as nothing* " to him compared
with slavery.

This being the case in the fullest sense of the
term, and slavery being an immutable fact, the
word "compromise" is not to be found in his
political vocabulary with regard to the slavery
question.   In a second speech on abolition petitions (February 6, 1837), he declares, "I hold
concession or compromise to be fatal. If we
concede an inch, concession would follow concession, compromise would follow compromise, until
our ranks would be so broken that effectual
resistance would be impossible." So as every

agitation of the slavery question in a hostile
spirit *eo ipso* touches the vitals of the "peculiar
institution," it must be suppressed, if the Union
is to be preserved. In the discussion of the
abolition petitions, his love of the Union had betrayed this slave of his own implacable logic
into the gross mistake of regarding the exclusion of the slavery question from the halls
of Congress as substantially identical with a
total and permanent extinction of its agitation
everywhere and in every form. He clung to
this fallacy, because to renounce it was to acknowledge that, if the rest of his argumentation
was correct, his attempts to save slavery *and*
the Union were *ab initio* absolutely idle. Now,
however, he did not recur to this point, but
drew directly from his premises the conclusion
that the Federal government was bound to effect the suppression of the agitation without
meddling in any way whatever with the "peculiar institution;" that is, that within the
sphere of its legitimate action, and to the fullest extent of its constitutional powers, it was
bound to do what the States demanded. No
justification for refusing to do so did or ever
could exist. Even the exercise of an unquestioned constitutional power was no valid excuse.
The discretion of Congress had its limit in the
notion of every single State as to what its indi-

vidual security demanded. A constitutional
Federal law would instantly lose its validity and
constitutionality, if a State should see fit, under
the plea of securing its peace, to pass a conflicting law : —

" The low must yield to the high ; the convenient
to the necessary ; mere accommodation to safety and
security. This is the universal principle which governs in all analogous cases, both in our social and political relations. Whenever the means of enjoying or
securing rights come into conflict, — rights themselves
never can, — this universal and fundamental principle
is the one which, by consent of mankind, governs in
all such cases. Apply it to the case under consideration, and need I ask which ought to yield ? Will
any rational being say that the laws of eleven States
of the Union which are necessary to their peace, security, and very existence ought to yield to the laws
of the general government regulating the post-office,
which at the best is a mere accommodation and convenience, — and this when the government was formed
by the States, mainly with a view to secure more perfectly their peace and safety ? But one answer can
be given. All must feel that it would be improper
for the laws of the States, in such case, to yield to
those of the general government, and of course that
the latter ought to yield to the former. When I say
ought, I do not mean on the principle of concession.
I take higher ground : I mean under the obligation of
the Constitution itself."

This obligation he found in the clause which empowers Congress "to make all laws which shall be necessary and proper for carrying into execution" the powers vested by the Constitution in the government of the United States, whence he drew the seemingly so simple and unanswerable conclusion that no law, relating to a mere accommodation and convenience, could be proper, if it endangered the peace, security, and very existence of any one of the States. Each State being the exclusive judge of what its peace and security demanded, the direct consequence was that each State had to decide upon the necessity and propriety of the Federal laws. Thus the final result of Calhoun's reasoning is again a systematization of anarchy, but it is an anarchy of a higher order than that which he had arrived at in the tariff controversy. Then he had claimed for each State the right to nullify, so far as itself was concerned, a Federal law which it deemed unconstitutional, and now he attributed to each State the right to invalidate a constitutional Federal law, and to render it unconstitutional by passing a conflicting law. Whether the law was to be invalidated only as to the particular State, or for the whole Union, we are not told. According to the theory, it ought to have been the former; but then the old difficulty arose, that there was a Federal law

which was a law but for a part of the Union,
while, if it was invalidated for the whole Union,
twenty-three sovereign States, which took no
exception to what their senators and representatives in Congress had seen fit to do, had to
submit to the will of one sovereign State.

We are not informed which horn of the di-
lemma Calhoun preferred; but in either case
the absurdity was so glaring that he again could
not have failed to see it, if, in the particular
matter on which he reasoned, there had not
been a solidarity of interests of all the slave-
holding States. This is the more evident as,
throughout the report and the speech, *each State*
and *the slave-holding States* are interchangeably
used as equivalent terms with regard to the
question in hand. The constitutional question
is argued in such a manner that the right and
the power claimed belong to each State individ-
ually; and whenever he came to speak of the
facts, that is to say, whenever he applied the
theory to the legislative problem before the
Senate, he said *the South, the eleven slave-holding States,* etc. In the report, too, as well as in
the speech, the consideration of the fact pre-
dominates in a very remarkable degree over the
constitutional argument : —

" He must be blind, indeed, who does not perceive
that the subversion of a relation which must be fol-

lowed with such disastrous consequences can only be
effected by convulsions that would devastate the country, burst asunder the bonds of the Union, and engulf,
in a sea of blood, the institutions of the country. It
is madness to suppose that the slave-holding States
would quietly submit to be sacrificed. Every consideration — interest, duty, and humanity, the love of
country, the sense of wrong, hatred of oppressors, and
treacherous and faithless confederates, and, finally,
despair — would impel them to the most daring and
desperate resistance in defence of property, family,
country, liberty, and existence."

Yes, it is madness to suppose that the slave-
holding States would quietly submit to be sacrificed, — *that* is the pivot on which the report,
the speech, and the bill turn, and not on any
clause of the Constitution. If "existence" was
at stake and "despair" sat at the council-table,
then, indeed, it was a matter of course that not
only the Union, but also the whole Constitution,
was "as nothing." Therefore, also, the speech
did not conclude with a maxim or rule of constitutional law, but with the announcement of a
fact: —

"I must tell the Senate, be your decision what it
may, the South will never abandon the principles of
this bill. If you refuse coöperation with our laws
and conflict should ensue between yours and ours, the
Southern States will never yield to the superiority of

yours. . . . Let it be fixed, let it be riveted, in every Southern mind that the laws of the slave-holding States for the protection of their domestic institutions are paramount to the laws of the general government in regulations of commerce and the mail; that the latter must yield to the former in the event of conflict."

In the opinion of those who neither saw nor thought beyond the immediate future, this announcement proved to be less than an empty threat. Not only was Calhoun's bill rejected, but in the same year another bill was passed by both Houses of Congress, and approved by the President, prohibiting postmasters, under severe penalty, from "unlawfully" detaining in their offices "any letter, package, pamphlet, or newspaper with intent to prevent the arrival and delivery of the same." Nowhere was the nullification of this law spoken of, and never again was an attempt made by Federal legislation thus indirectly to abridge the liberty of the press. Yet Calhoun was right in the most essential point. The South never did abandon the principle of this bill; that is to say, the principle that slavery had to be protected and defended at all hazards, — with and under the Constitution, if possible, but protected and defended it must and should be, under all circumstances and by any necessary means. Calhoun

knew that well enough, and he therefore did
not wear the dismayed mien of a defeated man.
With the same tone of deep, immutable conviction he repeated at every opportunity the
declaration that the South would never yield
in the slavery question, because it *could* not do
it. He did not live to see the day when this
declaration was put to its final test; but the delay was so long only because, through all these
gloomy years, the resistance of the North invariably broke down before the attacks of the
solid phalanx of the slave power. Calhoun had
been defeated in the question of the abolition
petitions and in that of the incendiary publications, because the South had not come up to the
mark; but the inglorious victories of the North
augured nothing but ignominious defeats for
the future, while Calhoun could anticipate brilliant — but alas, how terribly disastrous — victories, for he was sure that the South would
steadily advance towards the mark which he had
drawn for it. Therefore it would have been a
most egregious mistake to judge the situation by
the immediate result of his movement in those
two questions. The defeated " doctrinaire "
was not " shelved ; " on the contrary, his influence
was on the increase, though he dared once more
to throw the gauntlet into the face of public
opinion.

Nearly a year passed ere Calhoun addressed the Senate again on the slavery question. The old economical questions pushed themselves once more into the foreground. In spite of the compromise tariff, the revenues of the government increased at such a rate that the apprehension arose anew of seeing a vast surplus accumulate. The various propositions for averting that " calamity " or employing the superfluous money do not concern us here. It need only be mentioned that Calhoun considered it a serious danger, and as, in his opinion, the accumulation of the surplus could not be prevented, he earnestly advocated that it should be " deposited " in the treasuries of the States, according to their Federal representation.

It is a very curious and even important fact, which, so far as our knowledge goes, has thus far been entirely overlooked, that Calhoun, besides his general reasons, had a special purpose in proposing such a disposal of the surplus revenue. In a letter to some citizens of Athens, Georgia (August 5, 1836), he writes: —

" Instead of being cut off from the vast commerce of the West, as had been supposed, we find, to our surprise, that it is in our power, with proper exertions, to turn its copious stream to our own ports. Just at this important moment, when this new and brilliant prospect is unfolding to our view, the Deposit Bill is

about to place under the control of the States interested ample means of accomplishing, on the most
extended and durable scale, a system of railroad communication that, if effected, must change the social,
political, and commercial relations of the whole country vastly to our benefit, but without injuring other
sections."

The Federal government dares not do indirectly what it has no right to do directly — how
often had he declared this to be a fundamental
principle of constitutional law! And yet what
was this proposed distribution if not " internal
improvements" by indirection? True enough,
not internal improvements which Congress
deemed of national importance, but under the
exclusive control of the separate States, and intended, in the first place, to serve state interests.
But it is not because the consistency of Calhoun
might be called into question that this idea
deserves more attention than it has hitherto
received from historians. The arch-doctrinaire
was one of the first in the South to see that
with the railroads a force had been introduced
which was to exert a most powerful influence in
shaping the destinies of the country, not only in
general, but also with regard to the relation of
the two geographical sections lying respectively
north and south of Mason and Dixon's line.
He himself proposed a certain route through

the Alleghanies, spending eight days on his exploring expedition, and walking over a considerable part of the ground. The interest which he manifested in this problem was so great that the Southern papers spoke of him as the fittest man to be made the president of the great Southern and Western Railroad Company. He was fully awake to the importance of the fact that the difference in the wealth of the two sections increased every year in favor of the North; and he saw that, as the general economical development would go on at an unparalleled rate in consequence of communication by steam, this difference would necessarily increase at the same ratio if the South should lag behind the North in realizing the possibilities created by the new invention.   Yet his last conclusion could not have been more wrong, if every one of his premises had been erroneous.   Not Congress and its tariff laws, as he supposed, but slavery was the cause of the remarkable phenomenon which justly rendered him so uneasy; and therefore the new invention, which was a blessing to all mankind, was sure to prove a curse to the slave-holders.   As early as 1817 a representative of Louisiana had declared in Congress, "We need no roads;" and a country which needs no roads cannot have railroads. The will of the South was as nothing in this

question. The principal cities might indeed be
connected by rail, and it was done in the course
of time ; but there were, so to speak, no brooks
and rivers to feed the main streams, and, whatever the South might do, it could not create
them. The idea of Calhoun, to make up for
lost time and overtake the North by means of
railroads, was a more preposterous delusion than
any he had indulged in heretofore. No power
on earth could spur the South into a livelier
pace, because it is the very nature of the "peculiar institution" to move in a jog trot. The
railroads only served to put this fact into a more
glaring light; while in the North they accelerated the economical development more than the
wildest imagination could have anticipated at
that time.

It was neither all nor the worst that Calhoun's hopes were to be wholly disappointed,
and that a new impetus was to be given in the
direction in which the economical development
of the country had been moving ever since the
adoption of the Constitution. He was undoubtedly right in doing his best for an extensive
railroad system, for the less the South kept up
in this respect with the North the more unfa-
vorably would it compare in every respect with
the non-slave-holding States. But every spike
which fastened a rail in Southern soil was a

nail driven into the coffin of slavery; for every engine, nay, every traveller and every bale of goods, came impregnated with the spirit of the times, which would not and could not brook slavery. The South had no choice; Calhoun was right in believing that self-preservation bade the South to grasp even more eagerly than the North at the cup which was to mankind what the alchemists had vainly tried to find for the individual, — an elixir of life; but slavery turned it into poison. The irrepressible conflict between North and South was to end with the disruption of the Union; but another and more intense irrepressible conflict gnawed the intestines of the South, and it was this that rendered the doom of slavery inevitable. Whatever the merits or demerits of the deposit scheme were from a general point of view, if the Southern States should invest their share in railroads, it would certainly have been the best use they could make of the money, and yet it would have been better for them to throw all the surplus into the sea.

The adoption of Calhoun's device led to one of the most curious episodes in the financial history of the United States, which abounds with strange incidents. But whatever may be thought of the remedy, it will not be denied that Calhoun was right in asserting that the government ought not to take more out of the pockets of the citizens than it really needed for its legitimate purposes, and that a chronically plethoric treasury might have grave consequences. Calhoun chiefly apprehended that such a constantly overflowing purse would be a powerful means to corrupt the whole government machinery still more than heretofore, by leading to a further increase of the vast patronage of the Federal government, and by enlisting all the Federal officers still more exclusively in the party service, and that the independence and sovereignty of the States would thereby be still more endangered.

It had evidently become with him a matter of course that every legislative problem of a general character must, in some way or other, stand in close connection with these two questions. The alarming increase of the revenues was partly due to the enormous sales of the public lands, which were, to a great extent, bought on speculation. Here was certainly a problem of the first magnitude and beset with extraordinary difficulties; but it is, to say the least, rather surprising to see the greatest stress laid on the dangers which were to arise in those two respects from this source. This is not the place to discuss the great land question, and we will therefore not inquire into the merits or

demerits of Calhoun's general opinions concerning it. The reason for his proposition (February, 1837) to cede the public lands to the new
States, namely, "to place the senators and representatives from the new States on an equality
with those from the old, by withdrawing our
local control, and breaking the *vassalage* under
which they are now placed," would, however,
hardly admit of a serious criticism.

A less far-fetched opportunity was offered
him to discuss state sovereignty, from a new
point of view and in a thorough manner, in the
debate on the question of admitting Michigan
as a State. Congress had made the admission
dependent upon the condition that Michigan
should agree to a certain boundary line. This
agreement had been made, but opinions differed
as to whether it had been made in a legal or
illegal manner. As to the concrete question, it
suffices to say that Calhoun was of the latter
opinion. We have to look somewhat more
closely only at the general theory, which he
proclaimed on this occasion.

Calhoun asserted that the condition concerning the boundary attached "simply to her *admission* into the Union," and did not affect in
the least either the acceptance of her constitution by Congress or "the declaration that she
is a State." There was no difference of opinion

as to the first part of the assertion, but it was contended on the other side that Michigan was not and could not be a State before her admission into the Union. Calhoun proved that this assertion was incompatible with the act of Congress imposing the boundary condition. That, however, could not be decisive as to the main question. Contests upon great constitutional principles cannot be decided by appealing to the wording of a statute, because this might be grossly inaccurate and careless; besides, the Constitution would then be but a piece of wax in the hands of Congress, for Congress might at first pass a law to suit itself, and then declare the correct reading of the Constitution to be thus and thus, since this law says so and so. But Calhoun did not rest his case solely upon this act of Congress. He said : —

" I now go farther, and assert that it [the position of the friends of the bill before the Senate] is in direct opposition to plain and unquestionable matter of fact. There is no fact more certain than that Michigan is a State. She is in full exercise of sovereign authority, with a legislature and a chief magistrate. She passes laws; she executes them; she regulates titles, and even takes away life, — all on her own authority. Ours has entirely ceased over her; and yet there are those who can deny, with all these facts before them, that she is a State. They might as well deny the existence of this hall! "

If Calhoun had been able under any circumstances to consider a question of this nature with a judicial mind, instead of entering upon its examination with the foregone conclusions of a passionate partisan, he would have perceived at the first glance that the case was far from being so plain as he made it out. Michigan was unquestionably no longer a Territory, and she did — and she did *of right* — all that he had mentioned. The most appropriate — or it is perhaps more correct to say the least inappropriate — name to be found in the insufficient nomenclature of political science for the commonwealth, therefore, was possibly a "State." That, however, was of very little consequence with regard to the point made by Calhoun. Everything depended upon the answer to the question what *kind* of a State it was, or, in other words, what the term "State" signified in this particular case. That Michigan was not *at this moment* a State in the most general acceptation of the term, even Calhoun would hardly have ventured to deny. Would he have dared to assert that, while the question of her admission into the Union was pending, she would have the right to declare war against some other sovereign power, to conclude treaties, to coin money, to grant letters of marque and reprisal, etc.? Undeniably she lacked many of the most essential powers inherent to sovereignty, and, in consequence, she evidently was not a State as that phrase is most frequently used. Just as evidently she was not a State of the Union in the sense of the Constitution, for the question under consideration was her admission into the Union. Yet no one pretended that she was out of the Union. Whatever her legal relation towards the Federal government might be, she certainly was a part of the great commonwealth known by the name of the United States of America. Calhoun could the less contest this fact, because another proof which he adduced for his assertion was that Michigan had elected senators, and, according to the Constitution, only States elect senators. This argument clearly went too far the other way. In correct language, Michigan had not elected senators of the United States, but she had elected two men, who were to be her senators in Congress after she had been admitted into the Union. Also, since Michigan was a part of the republic, the authority of Congress over her had incontestably not " *entirely* ceased," for there is and can be no part of the republic over which Congress has not some authority. Whether this authority went so far as to give Congress the right to remand Michigan into her former territorial status, if she refused to comply with the conditions imposed upon her admission into the Union, need not here be inquired into. Calhoun's argument is like a sword without a blade, if it be proved that Michigan was but a State in an inchoate condition, which could be perfected only by the act of Congress admitting her into the Union.

Calhoun did, of course, not contest that an act of Congress was needed to make Michigan a State of the Union, but he did not assent any further to the proposition just stated.

"I am told, if this be so, if a Territory must become a State before it can be admitted, it would follow that she might refuse to enter the Union after she had acquired the right of acting for herself. Certainly she may. A State cannot *be forced* into the Union. She must come in *by her own free assent*, given in her highest sovereign capacity through a convention of the people of the State. Such is the constitutional provision; and those who make the objection must overlook both the Constitution and the elementary principles of our government, of which the right of *self-government is the first*, — the right of every people to form their own government, and to determine their political condition."

The right here claimed is not the right of secession. If secession, not as an eventually justifiable revolutionary act, but as a constitutional right, is a monstrous political absurdity, this

right thus asserted concerning Michigan is an
absurdity in comparison with which the right
of secession is the soundest political conception,
and even, like nullification, "a conservative
principle." Calhoun now and afterwards maintained that a so-called enabling act of Congress
was required to give a Territory the right to
erect itself into a State. But if any political
proposition can be called self-evident, it is certainly this: that an enabling act can only give
permission to a Territory to erect itself into
a State *of the Union*. Even if Congress could
ever be so regardless of duty, and so mad as to
give a Territory permission simultaneously with
adopting a state constitution to will itself out
of the Union, in which clause of the Constitution did this strict constructionist find the
power granted to Congress to commit such a
suicidal act? The Constitution, which Calhoun
proclaimed the grandest embodiment of political
wisdom thus far seen by the world, would have
been the greatest monstrosity ever conceived
by the human mind, if the Union could constitutionally lose all its territorial possessions,
merely because the inhabitants of the Territories
were pleased to bow themselves out of it, by
way of acknowledging the privilege accorded
them to become full members of the Union.
That "so long as these sound principles are ob-

served" no State would ever "reject this high privilege," or would "ever refuse to enter this Union," but rather would "rush into your embrace, so long as your institutions are worth preserving," was an assertion of no consequence whatever. The possibility stamps the theory as such an infinite absurdity that it would be an insult to the reader to discuss it at all, if John C. Calhoun had not been its advocate. But one month later he very correctly spoke of "the public domain" as being "the property of the whole people of the United States." So an insignificant minority — the inhabitants of the Territories — had the right to deprive the whole people of this inestimable property, and appropriate it exclusively to themselves, and, with the indirect sanction of Congress, given by the permission to adopt state constitutions, set up in business for themselves, without perhaps even deigning to say good-by to this Union, which improved so wonderfully upon the example of King Lear. But enough, and more than enough, of this doctrine, which every schoolboy will pronounce to be utter nonsense. Yet one of the most acute political reasoners produced by America honestly believed it, because it was a logical outgrowth of the doctrine of state sovereignty, and because the doctrine of state sovereignty was the sheet-anchor which held the worm-eaten bark of slavery to her moorings.

Poor man! Adams wrote some months later: "Calhoun looks like a man racked with furious passions and stung with disappointed ambition, as he is." Certainly, Calhoun had not forgotten his bitter disappointments, nor had he ceased to hope that he would, after all, some time reach the goal of his wishes; but his personal ambition had long ago become wholly subordinate to the passions which the slavery conflict had awakened in his bosom. The encroachments of the slave power upon the domain of liberty went on at an alarming rate; but Calhoun derived no satisfaction from any success, because every advance disclosed to his mind more clearly the immensity of the space still to be traversed, ere the slave-holders could say to themselves: Put out the watch-fires, let us rest and enjoy the fruits of our toils, for there is nothing more to be apprehended. In his second speech on the admission of Michigan, he had thus very correctly characterized himself: —

"It has perhaps been too much my habit to look more to the future and less to the present than is wise; but such is the constitution of my mind that when I see before me the indications of causes calculated to effect important changes in our political condition, I am led irresistibly to trace them to their sources, and follow them out in their consequences."

His name would appear in smaller letters in the history of the United States, but his happiness as a man would have been greater, if it had been otherwise. What wonder that passion raked its deep furrows into the face of a man who fought with all the fervor of his hot blood and all the energy of his iron will for a cause, and yet perceived that every victory gained increased the number and determination of its enemies, and rendered their ultimate triumph more probable, if not certain! If he had still been open to arguments on this head, this condition of the struggle would have necessarily awakened doubts in his mind concerning the justice of his cause; but as his stand had been irrevocably taken, the remarkable phenomenon had just the opposite effect. The denunciations of slavery by the abolitionists incited him to extol it in unmeasured terms.

In a brief but most important speech (February 6, 1837) the question of receiving the abolition petitions was taken up by him once more. It was not done with a view to a reconsideration of the memorable decision of the Senate, though he tried to prove that his opinion had been fully borne out by the course of events. He saw his prophecies about to be fulfilled, and his object was to warn the Senate once more to arrest its fatal course down the inclined plane, which terminated in an abyss.

"I then said that the next step would be to refer the petition to a committee, and I already see indications that such is now the intention. . . . We are now told that the most effectual mode of arresting the progress of abolition is to reason it down ; and with this view it is urged that the petitions ought to be referred to a committee. That is the very ground which was taken at the last session in the other House ; but instead of arresting its progress, it has since advanced more rapidly than ever. The most unquestionable right may be rendered doubtful if once admitted to be a subject of controversy, and that would be the case in the present instance."

This was all very true, but Calhoun was mistaken in supposing that it could be helped. In this very speech, he himself furnished the best proof that nothing, which either the Senate or any other earthly power could do, would alter any of these facts in the least. True enough, the attempt of the House of Representatives to reason abolitionism down had been worse than futile. The anti-slavery spirit *could not* be reasoned down ; and yet Calhoun's whole speech was nothing but an attempt to do this very thing, and to do it with arguments which unanswerably proved the truth of his first assertion, that it could *not* be done.

"They who imagine that the spirit now abroad in the North will die away of itself, without a shock or convulsion, have formed a very inadequate conception of its real character; it will continue to rise and spread, unless prompt and efficient measures to stay its progress be adopted. Already it has taken possession of the pulpit, of the schools, and, to a considerable extent, of the press, — those great instruments by which the mind of the rising generation will be formed.

"However sound the great body of the non-slaveholding States are at present, in the course of a few years they will be succeeded by those who will have been taught to hate the people and institutions of nearly one half of this Union with a hatred more deadly than one hostile nation ever entertained towards another. It is easy to see the end. By the necessary course of events, if left to themselves, we must become, finally, two peoples. It is impossible, under the deadly hatred which must spring up between the two great sections, if the present causes are permitted to operate unchecked, that we should continue under the same political system. The conflicting elements would burst the Union asunder, powerful as are the links which hold it together. Abolition and the Union cannot coexist. As the friend of the Union, I openly proclaim it, and the sooner it is known the better. The former may now be controlled, but in a short time it will be beyond the power of man to arrest the course of events."

What a bewildering tangle of contradictions!
If the anti-slavery spirit, left unchecked, was
sure to spread, and if it had already taken possession of the pulpit, of the schools, and of a
considerable part of the press, — that is to say,
of the three great formative agencies of public
opinion, — who and what should then check it?
Besides public opinion, there was no other power
except the public authorities. In a democratic
republic, however, the public authorities are the
creatures of public opinion, and not its masters.
And what did Calhoun want the public authorities to do? They were not to reason with the
anti-slavery spirit, for to argue the case at all
was to render the unquestionable right doubtful, and, as experience had taught, only served
the cause which was to be put down. Was
Congress to pass penal laws against the manifestation of the anti-slavery spirit in the pulpits, in the schools, and in the press? Would
not the mere suggestion of such a law raise a
storm of passionate debate, such as had never
before swept through the halls of Congress?
And if such laws could be passed in the face of
the express provisions of the Constitution and
against public opinion, how long could they remain in the statute-book? But if Congress
should not reason with the anti-slavery spirit,
and could not pass penal laws against it, what

could it do but maintain an indignant silence? Yet that would have been the policy of the ostrich. The danger does not disappear because we shut our eyes against it. Nobody knew this better than Calhoun, and so he spoke in tones which would have chilled the blood in the veins of his audience if they had had the faintest idea in what an awful manner every word of his predictions would be fulfilled in due time. Therefore it was, by his own showing, a delusion, without the smallest particle of firm ground to rest upon, that the anti-slavery spirit could yet be controlled. It was the natural offspring of the moral convictions and the political sentiments of the times; and, in consequence, every attempt to fetter it necessarily acted upon it as a spur. Calhoun could not have failed to understand that he had knocked the last vestige of his argument from under his feet, if it had not been so true that he spoke as a friend of the Union. Slavery had to be maintained though the skies should fall, yet that the days of the Union were numbered he would not believe until it was actually rent in twain. But abolition and this Union could not coexist; therefore there *had* to be some means of crushing abolitionism, though he himself had been forced to demonstrate that there was and could be none.

A man of so lucid a mind as Calhoun, and so incapable of consciously shutting his eyes to any truth because he did not like it, could not rest satisfied with being snugly spun into such a Gordian knot of contradictions. If it could not be unravelled, perhaps it might be cut by a bold stroke. The sword must, of course, be taken from the armory of reason. Did not the assertion that the anti-slavery spirit could not be reasoned down admit of a restrictive qualification? Denunciations, constitutional arguments, warnings, and threats were alike powerless. But could not the flood be stemmed, if the anti-slavery spirit were proved to be an egregious mistake and a gross blunder? This it was that he now undertook to do.

The Philadelphia Convention had nearly despaired of overcoming the difficulties thrown by slavery in the way of a "better Constitution," although the moral view taken of slavery by the North and the South differed at that time comparatively little. The more exacting the Southern States were with regard to slavery, the more readily did they admit that it was a moral, political, and economical evil. There was no hypocrisy in these declarations, though unquestionably the intensity of conviction did not generally correspond with the emphasis of language. The confessions would have been much more guarded if it had been apprehended that they might lead to disadvantageous consequences. Why should slavery not be called a mildew and a curse, since the North had no objection to having the whole responsibility for the existence of the evil thrown upon England, and since it was honestly believed that the prohibition of the foreign slave-trade would cause its gradual extinction? Was it not rather to be supposed that the resistance of the North against the demands of the South would be weakened by an appeal to the sympathy of Northerners with the unfortunate condition of their Southern brethren, and by strengthening the hope that the Southern States, prompted by their moral convictions and by what they considered their true interest, would make all possible exertions to render the constitutional compromises in favor of slavery only temporary make-shifts? The more these hopes proved to be vain delusions, the more it became the settled policy of the South to season its exactions with a strong dose of sound moral sentiments. The South had begun with honest self-deception, and it gradually sunk into conscious deception of others; hollow declamations took the place of true and more or less deep sentiments. Now and then a voice was heard energetically disclaiming the least hostility against negro slavery from any point of view. These bold confessions were, however, hardly noticed amid the din of general protestations against " slavery in the abstract," and though they were ominous signs of the times, they were, in fact, of themselves of no great importance, because they were after all but personal opinions. Only when placed on the basis of a general principle did they become a vital force, which pushed the slavery conflict into a new phase of development. Calhoun now took this decisive step, with full consciousness of its significance. He not only denied that slavery " in the abstract " was an evil, but he emphatically proclaimed negro slavery to be a good.

" But let me not be understood as admitting, even by implication, that the existing relations between the two races in the slave-holding States is an evil : far otherwise, I hold it to be a good, as it has thus far proved itself to be to both, and will continue to prove so if not disturbed by the fell spirit of abolition. . . . The relation now existing in the slave-holding States between the two [races] is, instead of an evil, a good, — a positive good."

The argument that the negroes were greatly benefited by slavery, because physically, intellectually, and morally their actual condition was infinitely better than it would have been in the wilds of Africa, was very old, and one still meets with it occasionally. Was it not, then, cruel and unchristian to declare the African slave-trade piracy, and thereby deprive the poor benighted Africans of every chance of undergoing this blissful change? But, however that might be, why was it a blessing for native-born Americans of the negro race to be kept in slavery, because it had been a blessing to their ancestors, two or more generations back, to be transported from Africa to America, though they were sold into slavery? But we need not dwell upon the threadbare sophistry of the argument, because Calhoun only repeated what had been said a thousand times before.

Of much more importance was his "appeal to facts" to support the other assertion: That slavery was also "a positive good" for the other race. "In the mean time," he said, "the white or European race has not degenerated. It has kept pace with its brethren in other sections of the Union, where slavery does not exist. It is odious to make comparisons; but I appeal to all sides whether the South is not equal in virtue, intelligence, patriotism, courage, disinterestedness, and all the high qualities which adorn our nature." Inefficient and unreliable as were the statistics of the United States at that time, they were full and accurate enough to tell a strange story about how the South had kept pace with

the North with regard to intelligence, so far as
intelligence depends upon school instruction and
upon the whole character of the life of the community in which an individual happens to live.
The history of the slavery conflict and of the
questions which stood in close connection with
it furnished an odd commentary on the peculiar disinterestedness of the South. Some parts
of the local news and the advertising columns
of the Southern papers concerning slaves were
strange reading for one wanting to inform himself about certain virtues and high qualities
which adorn our nature. Yet Calhoun spoke
in good faith, — only he had "the upper ten
thousand" in mind, while he spoke of the white
race. Every year it became more evident that
the curse of slavery weighed upon the white
race as heavily as upon the negroes, if not even
more so. Only in one thing did Calhoun admit
the inferiority of the South, — in "the arts of
gain:" a most important thing, indeed, since
the arts of gain are the most powerful agencies of civilization. But the South was not responsible for this one weak point in its case, for
he traced it "mainly to the fiscal action of this
government." Adam was more successful in
covering his nudity with a fig-leaf than the
South in the attempt to account for its unsat-
isfactory economical condition by this charge

against the economical policy of the Federal
government. Whether good or bad, that policy
had been the same for the whole country, and
the North had advanced with giant strides, while
the South, in spite of its natural advantages, its
cotton monopoly and the unparalleled increase
of the cotton culture, complained that "the fox
dwelt amid the hearth-stones of once blooming
plantations." There was no other essential difference in the condition of the two sections than
slavery and what had resulted from it, and to
slavery, therefore, the inferiority in the arts of
gain had ultimately to be traced.

This "appeal to facts" more than sufficed
to prove that heavy clouds, laden with storm
and lightning, overhung the sky of the sunny
South, if it adopted this doctrine of the positive
good of slavery to both races. For then it had
sealed with its own hands the decree of fate,
that it had steadily to go on from bad to worse.
But all this was as nothing compared with the
general principle, upon which Calhoun rested
his assertion: "I take higher ground. . . . I
hold, then, that there never has yet existed a
wealthy and civilized society in which one portion of the community did not, in point of fact,
live on the labor of the other." Almost in-
numerable have been the devices — "from the
brute force and gross superstition of ancient

times to the subtle and artful fiscal contrivances of modern " — by which so small a share of the wealth of all civilized communities has been allotted to those by whose labor it was produced, and so large a share given to the non-producing classes.

" I might well challenge a comparison between them and the more direct, simple, and patriarchal mode by which the labor of the African race is, among us, commanded by the European. I may say with truth that in few countries so much is left to the share of the laborer, and so little exacted from him. . . . But I will not dwell on this aspect of the question; I turn to the political, and here I fearlessly assert that the existing relation between the two races in the South, against which these blind fanatics are waging war, forms the most solid and durable foundation on which to rear free and stable political institutions. It is useless to disguise the fact. There is and always has been, in an advanced stage of wealth and civilization, a conflict between labor and capital. The condition of society in the South exempts us from the disorders and dangers resulting from this conflict; and explains why it is that the condition of the slave-holding States has been so much more stable and quiet than that of the North. The advantages of the former, in this respect, will become more and more manifest if left undisturbed by interference from without, as the country advances in wealth and numbers. We have,

in fact, but just entered that condition of society
where the strength and durability of our political institutions are to be tested; and I venture nothing in
predicting that the experience of the next generation
will fully test how vastly more favorable our condition of society is than that of other sections for free
and stable institutions, provided we are not disturbed
by the interference of others, or shall have sufficient
intelligence and spirit to resist promptly and successfully such interference."

This was a manifesto of infinitely more import than all his writings and speeches on nullification. His warfare against the anti-slavery
spirit had been in the beginning strictly defensive. Because the broad shield of the Constitution completely covered the " peculiar institution " of the South against all legislative
interference by the Federal government, therefore he had thought that it must also prove impenetrable to the arrows of abolitionism ; and
with the doctrine of state sovereignty he had
built the citadel of nullification, which would in
all emergencies furnish a last unconquerable re-
fuge. Strong as this position was, he soon became convinced that it was not strong enough.
Without abandoning it, he now warned the
North that the permanent and absolute security
of slavery was a question of life and death with
the South, and that this plain fact would deter-

mine its action, if the anti-slavery spirit was not promptly and forever crushed out. A constant warfare, calculated morally to ruin the slave-holding States in their own eyes and in the eyes of the civilized world, would not and could not be endured by them. Now he himself challenged not only the abolitionists, but the whole North and the whole civilized world, to a decisive combat with those moral and intellectual arms from which, according to his own statement, the slave-holding States alone had anything to apprehend, — a most audacious but unavoidable step. If a successful defence was at all possible, the attack had to be met with the same weapons with which it was made. As long as the South apologized for slavery as a dire necessity, a vast majority of the Northern people would insist upon having the constitutional obligations scrupulously fulfilled by the Federal government. But they would do it less and less willingly, because the anti-slavery spirit, which was the spirit of the times, could not be checked by the Constitution ; for the Constitution was a rule of *action*, but not a law for the thoughts and sentiments of the people. If the hostile feeling against slavery was to be conquered, the people had to be convinced that it was mistaken and wrong. And as slavery could not be an indifferent thing, if its maintenance was a ques-

tion of life and death with the South, it must necessarily be a blessing.   Thus the necessities of
defence imperatively demanded the transforma-
tion of slavery from a curse into a most enviable
institution, for moral and political reasons.

That there was some truth in Calhoun's assertions could not be gainsaid.   The conflict
between labor and capital constituted the significance of the times in the western world,
and the slave-holding States knew nothing of it,
because labor was owned by capital, and therefore capital arranged the relation in every respect wholly to suit itself.   So long as labor did
not appeal to brute force, the South was, in consequence, exempt from the dangers and disorders which result from this conflict in communities where labor, too, has its rights and is in a
condition to defend its interests ; there it was
navigation on a pond, here on a never motion-
less and sometimes tempestuous sea ; but there
the sun bred poisonous miasmas in the stagnant
waters, and the navigator was in danger of suffo-
cating in the mire if the boat capsized by some
accident, while here were the dangers, but also
the vigor and all the resources, of real, ever progressing life.   Had Calhoun so entirely forgotten
all that he had seen during his college years in
New England that this difference really escaped
his keen eye ?   Had he grown to be so impreg-

nated with the spirit of slavery that the spirit of
the people of the free States had become to him
a book closed with seven seals? Could they ever
be made to believe that slavery was "a positive
good"? And if this declaration would always
have the sound of a blasphemy in their ears,
what would he have gained for the security of
slavery in the Union, even if his assertion were
true? The hatred of slavery in the North was
as yet very far from being so deadly as he expected it to become in a little while; but still
slavery was hated upon political, moral, and
religious principles. Principles, however, are
vital forces in the history of mankind, and what
a man believes to be a principle works with him
as such. Therefore, even if Calhoun were right,
his declaration could only fan the flames of the
conflict between South and North. It was the
formal announcement that this conflict never
could terminate in a peace, nor even be inter-
rupted by an honest truce.

All the free States were genuine democracies,
and therefore the assertion that slavery is the
most solid and durable foundation upon which
to rear free institutions was in their eyes simply
a *contradictio in adjecto*. Whether the institutions which the South reared on this base were
good or bad, they were confessedly the products
of a different civilization, — of a civilization dif-

fering from that of the North not only in details,
but in the formative principle. It is, however,
self-evident that two civilizations, with antagonistic formative principles, cannot permanently
coexist in one political organism, because they
move in opposite directions. Instead of recon-
ciling the North and the civilized world to the
existence of slavery, Calhoun's new gospel of
slavery was a declaration of aggressive war.
But one step more could be taken in this direction : the deeds could be made to conform to the
theory, the conversion of the heathen to the new
gospel could be undertaken ; the logical consequence of the doctrine of the " positive good "
was the propagandism of slavery.

The time was not far off when the South,
with Calhoun as its foremost leader, was to take
this last step, which proved to be the beginning
of the end. For a while, however, the attention
of the country was diverted from the slavery
conflict by financial and other economical questions, which pressed themselves into the foreground in a most unpleasant manner.

We have seen how many wise heads in the
Capitol at Washington, and among them that
of Calhoun, were troubled by the fear that the
United States government stood in danger of
something like the fate of King Midas. But
instead of having to deal with an overflowing

treasury, they had to struggle with the disastrous consequences of the crash of 1837, the
worst economical crisis the country had as yet
experienced since the war of independence. Calhoun took a prominent but not a leading part
in all the questions mediately and immediately
connected with this catastrophe. To present
the reader with an intelligent synopsis of his
views would require a discourse on the general
history of the times, which cannot be com-
pressed within the small frame of this biography. It appears, however, the less necessary to
enlarge upon them, because no new principles
were involved in the discussion, and the stand
taken by Calhoun did not mark a new epoch in
his general career. From the personal point of
view it is almost of more interest that, in February, 1837, he had a last direct encounter with
General Jackson, who had taken him to task
for some remarks supposed to have been made
by Calhoun in a speech on the land question.
As the hot-tempered President had based his
grossly abusive letter on an inaccurate report,
Calhoun had no difficulty in chastising him severely for this attempt " upon the privileges of
a United States senator ; " this time, however,
himself overstepping the limits which the official station of his adversary should have imposed upon him.

Perhaps this incident influenced to some extent his language in the speech which he delivered a few days later on the relations of the United States to France ; but it would be ridiculous to suppose that personal hostility to Jackson was the reason of his opposition to the policy of the President in the indemnity question. He proved beyond contradiction that the untoward turn which this affair had taken was mainly due to the false steps of the administration, and he conclusively showed that in a war between the United States and France the former would have infinitely more to suffer, while neither could derive any advantage from it. The national pride was flattered to hear the victor of New Orleans blow the war trumpet so lustily and defiantly ; but the sober second thought of the people entirely agreed with Calhoun, that it would be madness, on a mere question of " etiquette," to provoke a war with the oldest ally of the United States, who had rendered them such signal services in their hour of need.

CHAPTER VII

UNDER VAN BUREN

Much time was to elapse ere justice was rendered Calhoun with regard to the course he saw fit to pursue upon the leading question of the day, — President Van Buren's sub-treasury scheme, which was to sever entirely and forever the connection between the government and banks of every description. It was but natural that the Whigs were deeply chagrined to see Calhoun part company with them in the moment when, as he himself freely admitted, the continuation of the alliance would have led to the overthrow of the administration party; but they had no right to expect anything else from him. He was not guilty of any treachery, nor could he be justly charged with inconsistency, though in 1835, when the sub-treasury scheme was first introduced by General Gordon, he had declared it " premature," and in 1836, when the proposition was renewed by Benton, " impracticable at the time ; " nay, even though he had himself proposed the establishment of a United States Bank for twelve years " as a

better and more practical plan to unbank the
banks." It accorded strictly with the facts
when he declared, "We joined our old opponents on the tariff question, but under our own
flag and without merging in their ranks." Nobody had ever pretended that he had become a
Whig; he had concluded an alliance with the
Whigs for the specific purpose of opposing the
encroachments of the Executive upon the domain of the other departments of government,
and of counteracting all the dangerous tendencies of Jackson's unscrupulous autocratic rule.
From Martin Van Buren, however, nothing was
to be apprehended. "Executive usurpation
had been arrested. The Treasury was empty,
and the administration had scarcely a majority
in either House or in the Union." The object
of the alliance had been accomplished. The
questions which were now the order of the day
left the two great national parties intact, but
Calhoun was free to join either side, because
he belonged to neither. "He was master of
his own move, and acknowledged connection
with no party but the state-rights party, — the
small band of nullifiers, — and acted either with
or against the administration or the national
party, just as it was calculated to further the
principles and policy which we, of that party,
regarded as essential to the liberty and insti-

tutions of the country." Viewing the general
situation of the country in the manner he did,
it was therefore a matter of course that he
pitched his solitary tent for the present next
the camp-fires of the administration party.

"We have, Mr. President, arrived at a remarkable
era in our political history. The days of legislative
and executive encroachments, of tariffs and surpluses,
of bank and public debt and extravagant expenditure,
are past for the present. The government stands in
a position disentangled from the past, and freer to
choose its future course than it has ever been since
its commencement. We are about to take a fresh
start. I move off under the states-rights banner,
and go in the direction in which I have been so long
moving. I seize the opportunity thoroughly to reform the government; to bring it back to its original
principles; to retrench and economize; and rigidly
to enforce accountability. I shall oppose strenuously all attempts to originate a new debt; to create
a national bank; to reunite the political and money
powers (more dangerous than church and state) in
any form or shape; to prevent the disturbances of the
compromise, which is gradually removing the last
vestige of the tariff system. And, mainly, I shall use
my best efforts to give an ascendency to the great
conservative principle of state sovereignty over the
dangerous and despotic doctrine of consolidation."

Had the Whigs, then, quite overlooked that,
although he had fought with them against Jack-

son, it was an utter impossibility that he should ever exert himself for their ascendency? That the man who declared that he "wished to be considered nothing more than a plain and an honest *nullifier*" should "join the friends of the tariff, of a national bank, and the whole system of congressional usurpations, and utterly break down his old friends of 1827, who had taken shelter under his position, and thus give a complete and final victory to his old opponents of that period, and with it a permanent ascendency to them and their principles and policy, which, he honestly believed, could not but end in consolidation, with the loss of our liberty and institutions," — this, indeed, was a most preposterous idea. Calhoun, however, was mistaken in one point, and that the most material. The victory of the administration could never turn to the advantage of the states-rights party. The independent Treasury gave the administration of the finances a really political character for the first time, and it therefore necessarily contributed to the growing together of the "sovereign" States into a national Union.

Our sources do not inform us whether Calhoun ever became aware of this fact. His first great movement to bring the government "back to its original principles" looks less like the hopeful beginning of a thorough reform than like the

desperate effort of a man who is in danger of
being swallowed up by the surging waves, to pile
up dike upon dike till he has a wall so broad
and high that he can laugh the most furious
storms to scorn. Vain exertions, for his dikes
are not constructed of earth, stone, and mortar,
but of mere assertions. The most strenuous
efforts of the North to put down abolitionism by
public opinion had been met by the South with
the contemptuous remark that all the satisfaction the South got for its just complaints was
"words, mere words;" and now the great
leader of the slave power had nothing more
substantial to throw into the way of the anti-
slavery spirit than "words, mere words." The
last aim and end of the bringing back of the
government to its original principles was the
security of slavery; and this was to be obtained
not by legislation, but by *resolving* this and that
with regard to the constitutional and political
aspect of the slavery question. Did these long
strings of resolutions, by being spread over the
journal of the Senate, acquire any secret virtue
which made them a wall of adamant, against
which all the arms of the anti-slavery spirit
would splinter like glass? Whom did they
bind? Not even the Senate itself, and yet
infinitely less the other departments of the
government or even the people. They had no

legal authority whatever, and though they might be of great moral weight with many persons, what effect was to be expected from the mere opinion of the temporary majority of the Senate, which might be changed at any moment, if all the bulwarks of the Constitution were no longer deemed in themselves sufficient protection for the peculiar institution? Surely, the resolution mania, which from this time possessed Calhoun, is alone ample proof how justly he was charged with being a doctrinaire.

But it was a great mistake to suppose that all the weeks which the haughty planter forced the Senate, at the expense of its legitimate legislative business, to pass in debate on his constitutional opinions were spent to no purpose. It has been said before that, with regard to the slavery question, this doctrinaire was the only one who moved on at even pace with the events, and he knew now as well as ever what he was about. So far as he expected anything from his resolutions for the greater security of slavery he was not only disappointed, but he did in fact, as he was charged on all sides with doing, pour oil upon the flames. But the resolutions were not only designed to serve as additional guards for the " positive good " of the South; they were besides a programme for the future, and as such they were a political event of the first magnitude.

The central idea of the resolutions of December 27, 1837, was, of course, that the safety of the South depended entirely upon the doctrine of state sovereignty, and their immediate purpose was to get the Senate formally pledged to this principle in its direct bearings on the slavery question. Hence the series was very logically opened by stating how the Union *came into existence* under the Constitution. It is declared that every State " *entered* into the Union" by its own voluntary act. The old Union under the Articles of Confederation, therefore, evidently had ceased to exist some time before; when and how, Calhoun unfortunately forgot to say. The Senate, however, with thirty-one against thirteen votes, assented to this bold falsification of a plain historical fact.

This premise once secured, Calhoun had won the game. From the purely Confederate nature of the Union the second resolution was deduced : that the intermeddling of States or of a " combination of their citizens with the domestic institutions or police of the others, on any ground, or under any pretext whatever, political, moral, or religious, with a view to their alteration or subversion," is " not warranted by the Constitution." Pompous and positive as this resolution sounded, it was of so gelatinous a character that, while the political agitator could do

anything he pleased with it, the constitutional
jurist could not keep the smallest particle of it
firmly between his fingers. Who was able to
enumerate " the domestic institutions " to which
the doctrine of the resolution could be rightfully
applied? Webster showed conclusively that
slavery, for one, did not belong to them. Where,
too, was the master mind which could give a
serviceable definition of " intermeddling," or of
" with a view to their alteration," or of " not
warranted by the Constitution " ? If all this
was to have so precise a meaning that the
doctrines of rights should and could be fixed in
laws, and their observance secured by compulsory
legal measures, — and it was, obviously, only on
this supposition that they could serve the purpose
intended, — then everything which had relation
to the domestic institutions of other States would
become a punishable violation of the Constitution.
The existence of slavery had to vanish from the
consciousness of the free States; for until this
happened their thoughts must be in some degree occupied with it; the thoughts must manifest themselves, and every manifestation of the
thoughts had, in and of itself, a tendency to
operate an " alteration " of the existing state of
things. Yet the resolution served well enough
Calhoun's main purpose. What this was, he
plainly told in his rejoinder to the suggestion to

strike out the word "religious," — that "the whole spirit of the resolution hinged on that word." The Senate was to declare that the anathema of the Constitution rested on the heads of the fanatics who presumed to question the rightfulness of negro slavery on moral and religious grounds; and the Senate complied with the demand; only fourteen out of forty-five votes being recorded in favor of striking out the words "moral" and "religious." But what had Calhoun gained by that, even supposing that his interpretation of the spirit of the Constitution was correct? Would the religious convictions of the people be subverted by the Constitution, or would the latter become a dead letter from the moment when it stood in acknowledged antagonism to the former? Always there was the same fundamental error in all his reckoning. He clearly perceives that the whole slavery question hinges upon the political, economical, and moral antagonism between slavery and liberty, tries to suppress some *manifestations* of it, and draws from that suppression conclusions, as if it were identical with the suppression of the antagonism itself. But the futility of his efforts has pressed him another step forward: instead of merely forbidding the agitation to enter the Capitol, he now bids Congress declare that the Constitution wants to see every door in the free States hermetically closed against it.

To understand the whole import of the second resolution it is, however, necessary to read it in connection with the third, which indirectly overthrew the demand of the former, but of course in favor of slavery. This third resolution declared it to be the duty of the Federal government to use its powers in such a manner as " to give . . . increased stability and security to the domestic institutions of the States that compose the Union." The people of the free States were to have no political, moral, or religious thoughts on slavery, or at least not to manifest them in any way whatever disagreeable to the slave-holding States; but they were bound, through the Federal government, actively to exert themselves in its favor. It is not said in what manner and to what extent this was to be done; but did not the very generality of the terms used imply that it had to be done in *any* manner and to *any* extent declared necessary by the slave-holding States? For they alone had the right to judge what the stability and security of their peculiar institution demanded. There was not a trace of doctrinarian spirit in *this* resolution. It was a positive programme, big with consequences which would have curdled the blood in the veins of Calhoun himself, if he had foreseen them *all*. It was the first step towards deriving the practical results of the doctrine of the "positive good;" the first step towards securing the services of the Federal government for the glorious work of slavery propagandism.

The fourth resolution applied the foregoing doctrines by name to slavery, declaring all attacks on it "a manifest breach of faith, and a violation of the most solemn obligations, moral and religious." The Senate called upon to instruct the people in this spirit about their religious obligations; abolition, according to Calhoun, in possession of the pulpits, the schools, and the press; the abolitionists declaring slavery "the sum of all villainies," — was anything more needed to prove that two antagonistic principles were here in deadly conflict? With this one line Calhoun had irrefutably demonstrated the vanity of all his efforts to save slavery and the Union.

The next resolution read, —

"Resolved, That the intermeddling of any State or States, or their citizens, to abolish slavery in this District, or in any of the Territories, on the ground or under the pretext that it is immoral or sinful, or the passage of any act or measure of Congress with that view, would be a direct and dangerous attack on the institutions of all the slave-holding States."

If all that had been asserted in the preceding resolutions was correct, this one was certainly incontrovertible; therefore it was all the more significant that Calhoun refrained from declaring the abolition of slavery in the District of Columbia unconstitutional, although he expressly stated this to be his opinion. But while he thus politely and obligingly bowed to the constitutional doctrines of the North, its moral and religious convictions were once more imperiously bidden to leave this question alone. "The deluded agitators must be plainly told that it is no concern of theirs what is the character of our institutions." Not a finger was to be raised against slavery "under the pretext" of its immorality or sinfulness, not only where it actually existed, but also, added the sixth and last resolution, where it *might* exist in future.

"To refuse to extend to the Southern and Western States any advantage which would tend to strengthen or render them more secure, or to increase their limits or population by the annexation of new territory or states, on the assumption or under the pretext that the institution of slavery, as it exists among them, is immoral or sinful, or otherwise obnoxious, would be contrary to that equality of rights and advantages which the Constitution was intended to secure alike to all the members of the Union."

One great merit this last resolution had: its language was so plain that no child could misunderstand it. The principle of slavery pro-

pagandism was proclaimed with the utmost boldness, and the Federal government was absolutely
denied the right to interfere with it on any
ground or pretext connected in any way whatever with slavery. Not to interfere was, however, in this case, identical with an obligation to
lend a helping hand, for " the annexation of new
territory or states " could be effected only by the
Union. And why should the Union not exult-
ingly march on under the black flag of slavery
as far as the South was good enough to lead it?
It is true, " many in the South once believed that
it was a moral and political evil," but " that folly
and delusion are gone. We see it now in its
true light, and regard it as the most safe and
stable basis for free institutions in the world.
. . . The blessing of this state of things extends beyond the limits of the South. It makes
that section the balance of the system; the
great conservative power, which prevents other
portions, less fortunately constituted [!], from
rushing into conflict." Verily, here is a doctrinaire with a positiveness in his doctrines
powerful enough to grind into dust the columns of the most gigantic political edifice. Not
long ago Calhoun had declared that nothing
was needed to render the South perfectly safe
save concert of will and action. Now, Providence had thrown ample opportunities into the

way of the Union to test whether that was sufficient to cajole and whip the North into obedience, and to force upon it this programme of the slave power, which, by the very consciousness of its hopeless weakness, was under the imperious necessity of rendering itself the despotic master of the Union, in order to save itself.

After this great sally, several years passed ere Calhoun thought it opportune to make the next decisive move in the cause of self-government and republican liberty on the basis of slavery. The waves of party strife rolled high during all these years, and Calhoun was far from being an unconcerned and idle spectator. His speeches of this period fill a stately volume, and are fully on a level with his other parliamentary efforts on general legislative topics. Yet the biographer, who confines himself to what is really characteristic of the man or to what has exerted a determining influence on the history of his country, can pass them over with a few general remarks. What he himself said of the extraordinary session of Congress in 1841 applies, so far as he is concerned, to this whole time. " What are we doing, and what engrosses all our attention from morn to noon, and from week to week, ever since our arrival here at the commencement of this extraordinary session, and will continue till its end? What but banks,

loans, stocks, tariffs, distribution, and supplies? "
The old economical controversies, more or less
altered by circumstances, are the battle-ground of
the parties, fighting with undiminished ardor and
varying success. The old arguments are repeated
ad nauseam. Though all the questions were of
the highest importance, and much erudition, ingenuity, eloquence, and passion were displayed
on both sides, the continuous reading of the
debates is simply treadmill work. Calhoun's
speeches, too, abound with repetitions. The sta-
tistical data, the illustrations, the arrangement
of the thoughts, change; but he fights for his
old doctrines with the old reasons: independent
treasury, no bank, no internal improvements, no
protective tariff, no distribution of the proceeds
of the sale of the public lands, cession of the
public lands to the States in which they are situated, no loans, etc. A good deal of sound reasoning, a good deal of bold and sometimes reckless generalizing, now and then exaggerated into
a downright absurdity, may be found in all his
speeches on these interesting subjects. The
thorough student of the general history of the
United States cannot dispense with perusing
them all carefully, but they do not show either
the man or the statesman in a new light. From
the personal point of view, they are the most
interesting on account of some sharp encounters

which he had with Clay and Webster. Each
of the three great senators tried to demonstrate
his own consistency throughout his political career, and the inconsistency which had marked
that of his adversary ; and each of them was perfectly successful as to the latter task, and, in
spite of infinite ingenuity and eloquence, sadly
failed as to the former. With the change
of conditions, their political convictions had
changed, and, by changing these, they had
learned to read the Constitution in a different
way. Neither of them lost anything in the estimation of the people by this fact, because it
was an honest change of opinion, and since their
constituents had gone through the same process
they might have had the manliness and candor
to avow it unreservedly. But perhaps the reproach that not one of them ventured upon a
standpoint of such moral elevation rests more
upon the general tendency of American politics
than upon them personally. Once, indeed, Calhoun openly confessed that he had been originally
inclined to take a latitudinarian and national
view of the powers of the Federal government ;
but when he spoke in the deep and incisive
tones of an authority, — and that became more
and more his habitual way of speaking, — or
when an opponent had nettled his self-love, he
was but too easily betrayed into wasting his

time and his ability in vain attempts to knead
his earlier sayings and political acts into the
mould of his present convictions.

Some of the speeches of this period require
particular notice, but they are precisely those
which were only remotely or not at all connected with the party issues.

The illegitimate connection of the civil service with party politics had become such a cry-
ing evil that another effort was made to strike
it at the root; but again the would-be reformers sought the root where it did not lie. A bill
was introduced and debated upon, which, as
Calhoun expressed it, proposed " to inflict the
penalty of dismission on a large class of the officers of this government, who shall electioneer,
or attempt to control or influence the election
of public functionaries either of the general or
state governments, without distinguishing between their official and individual character as
citizens."   Calhoun, who spoke on the bill on
February 22, 1839, declared it for this reason
unconstitutional.   We need not inquire whether
this charge was well founded, or whether he
made good his case as to the constitutional question.   Supposing that he was right, this defect
of the bill could have been easily mended; but
he very justly asserted that such a law would
" prove either useless, or worse than useless."

"But suppose the immediate object of the bill accomplished, and the office-holders rendered perfectly silent and passive, it might even then be doubted whether it would cause any diminution in the influence of patronage over elections. It would indeed greatly reduce the influence of the office-holders. They would become the most insignificant portion of the community, as far as elections were concerned. But just in the same proportion as they might sink, the no less formidable corps of the office-seekers would rise in importance. The struggle for power between the *ins* and the *outs* would not abate in the least, in violence or intensity, by the silence or inactivity of the office-holders, as the amount of patronage, the stake contended for, would remain undiminished. Both sides, those in and those out of power, would turn from the passive and silent body of the incumbents, and court the favor of the active corps, that panted to supplant them ; and the result would be an annual sweep of the former, after every election, to make room to reward the latter, — and this on whichever side the scale of victory might turn. The consequence would be rotation with a vengeance. The wheel would turn round with such velocity that anything like a stable system of policy would be impossible. Each temporary occupant, who might be thrown into office by the whirl, would seize the moment to make the most of his good fortune, before he might be displaced by his successor, and a system (if such it might be called) would follow, not less corrupting than unstable."

That was all true enough, but what had he to propose instead ? " Place the office-holders, with their yearly salaries, beyond the reach of the executive power, and they would in a short time be as mute and inactive as this bill proposes to make them. Their voice, I promise, would then be scarcely raised at elections, or their persons be found at the polls." If he had changed but one word, — if he had said *party in power* instead of *executive power*, — this advice would, indeed, have been the egg of Columbus. The context hardly allows a doubt that he now, as before, only wished to assign a controlling influence over the removals to Congress or the Senate ; and if that was to be the whole reform, his law, like the bill under discussion, would have been " useless, or worse than useless." As concerning the slavery conflict, so also in this question, he foresaw and foretold the impending dangers and inevitable evil consequences, and he showed great ability in criticising the opinions of the other political physicians ; but his own prescriptions were poisonous drugs.

In respect to the civil service, this is not very surprising, because, though Calhoun saw clearer than most of his contemporaries, he had after all not made a serious effort to push his examination beyond the surface of the question ; another generation was to grapple with this problem, for it had to grow infinitely worse ere the necessity of getting at the bottom of it could be fully realized. But of the slavery conflict he had a better right than anybody to say, as he frequently did, that he had thoroughly examined it in all its bearings, and that he understood it. Therefore the apodeictic manner in which he promised a radical cure, if but the application of his remedies would be consented to, exposes him to the charge of having been a dishonest quack, if he is not admitted to have been an honest fanatic, who, like all fanatics, viewed his subject but from one fixed point and under one unchangeable visual angle.

This deep conviction of his own infallibility in relation to everything concerning slavery rendered it a very significant fact that he once was compelled to admit that he was at his wits' end, and had no advice to offer. Of course neither pride nor policy allowed the very words to fall from his lips, but the folded arms and knitted brow with which, after reiterated loud complaints, he suffered the government to remain in the embarrassing situation, into which it had been thrown by trying to serve the interests of the slave-holders, spoke with a most impressive eloquence.

Two American vessels with negroes on board, the Comet and the Encomium, had been

stranded, in 1830 and 1834, on the false keys
of the Bahama Islands, and the local authorities
of Nassau, New Providence, had refused to recognize the negroes as slaves and deliver them
up to their owners. In 1835 a very similar case
occurred. The brig Enterprise was forced by
stress of weather into Port Hamilton, Bermuda, and the local authorities detained the
slaves, pretending that they had become freemen by coming within English jurisdiction.
The United States government took up all
three cases in behalf of the owners, and claimed
a fair compensation. England at last yielded
as to the first two, but persisted in her refusal
as to the last, and, at the same time, declared
that no such claim would ever again be allowed.
This distinction was based upon the fact " that
before the Enterprise arrived at Bermuda slavery
had been abolished in the British Empire."

On March 4, 1840, Calhoun introduced in
the Senate a set of resolutions declaratory of
what he conceived to be the principles of the
law of nations applying to the case, and severely
condemning the course of the English authorities. Some days later he delivered a long
speech in support of the resolutions, and had
the satisfaction of seeing them unanimously
adopted. The South liked to dwell upon this
fact as a striking proof of the justice of its

claims.   The unanimity of the Senate was, however, only apparent.   Of fifty-two senators, only
thirty-three voted; nineteen were evidently not
satisfied that Calhoun had made good his case,
but for reasons best known to themselves they
preferred not to say so.   The "unanimous"
vote of the Senate was, in fact, a proof of the
awe in which almost all the Northern politicians stood of the slave power, but there was
very little reason to draw from it the conclusion that the doctrine propounded in the resolutions could not be called into question.   Adams,
who certainly knew as much of the law of nations as any member of Congress, wrote concerning the Enterprise resolutions, "Calhoun
crows about his success in imposing his own
bastard law of nations upon the Senate by his
preposterous resolutions, and chuckles at Webster's appealing to those resolutions now, after
dodging from the duty of refuting and con-
founding them then."

The essential point of Calhoun's doctrine was
that he denied the right of England, with regard to citizens of foreign countries, to make
any difference between slaves and other property, if by some unavoidable cause the slaves
should momentarily come within the limits of
her jurisdiction.   This opinion was based upon
the assertion that slavery was fully recognized

by the law of nations. England did not directly
and in so many words assert the contrary, but
she proved by her acts that, at least so far as
any positive obligations could be deduced from
this principle, she refused to acknowledge its
existence or its binding force upon her. This
fact was in itself proof absolute that Calhoun's
assertion could at best be true only with a most
important qualification. He overlooked the fact
that the law of nations is not immutable, but
constantly changing and developing with the
general development of civilization. The very
fact that England assumed the position she did
sufficiently proved that this law was in a state
of transition as to the principle in question.
The law of nations rests upon the free consent
of the civilized peoples. If, therefore, the greatest maritime power of the world, with most extensive possessions adjacent to the sea or surrounded by it in all parts of the globe, withdrew
its assent to a principle of which the practical
application was confined to the seacoast, it
could no longer be maintained. That this was
so with regard to the case in hand was the more
evident, because none of the other European
powers of any consequence had a practical interest in the question, and the hostility of public opinion all over the civilized world against
slavery was constantly and rapidly increasing.

Calhoun's resolutions, therefore, were neither more nor less than a vain protest against the onward course of civilization, and the Senate, by " unanimously " adopting them, announced to the world that the most democratic and most progressive state of the universe was bound to cry Halt! and pull back the wheel of time whenever and wherever the interests of the slave-holders were in danger of being crushed by it.

To oblige the slave power, the Senate had made an ugly blot on the record of the United States, and the slave power did not derive the least advantage from it, nay, it even sustained positive damage. England did not change her course by a single point on account of the resolutions, and the attention of the world had again been called in the most pointed manner to the allegation that slavery was indeed a " positive good " and the best foundation of liberty. That *was* a positive damage, and no small one, for every syllable of what Calhoun had said years ago, with such impressive emphasis about the part played by the moral convictions in the tragedy of this conflict, was true. Every such manifestation of the slave power caused its opponents to write with larger letters on their own banner the device under which the slavocracy had been sailing ever since the adoption

of the Constitution : Let us alone ! Slavery is a
state institution with which the Federal government has no concern. Let us alone! To be
left alone in this sense was, however, to be
delivered over to destruction by the moral and
economical agencies which rule the world. The
" Let us alone " of the slave-holders meant,
You have not only to shut your eyes and ears,
but also to lock up your thoughts and your consciences, whenever our interests require you to
do so ; for slavery is a domestic institution of
the sovereign States ; but it is your duty to
throw the whole weight of the Union for us
into the scales, whenever we tell you that our
safety demands it, for the Constitution recog-
nizes and " guarantees " slavery. How long
would the North submit to such a bargain?
That question nobody could answer as yet; but
two things were certain : every time that the
Federal government submitted to its enforce-
ment, the number of those in the North who
grew restive under it increased ; and every time
that the slave-holders had succeeded in enfor-
cing it, they were compelled to push *both* sides
of their claim a long step farther. Calhoun,
understanding the nature of the slavery question better than any other Southern man, had
to march far ahead on both diverging lines, and
therefore, while no other single man has done

so much to erect the temple of the slave power, also no other single man has done so much to render its sudden downfall inevitable and to hasten the catastrophe. So it was in this case. What a triumph that not a single senator dared to raise his voice against the "bastard law of nations," and what a portentous humiliation to have nothing but "words, words, and again words" to oppose to England's "outrageous course"! The South pocketed at the same time the glorious impotent resolutions and a signal defeat.

There is no question that Calhoun very keenly felt the defeat, for he had declared that a "vital principle" was involved for the South, and that England "interdicted nearly as effectually the intercourse by sea between one half of this Union and the other, as to the greatest and most valuable portion of the property of the South, as if she was to send out cruisers against it." Yet he soon scrupulously avoided touching upon the question even in private conversation. But he deemed the success which he had obtained over the North of more import, for the obvious reason that the fate of the slave power depended not upon the international, but upon the national, standing of slavery. In November, 1841, the English authorities of Nassau dared to repeat their former offence under

were not based upon their cheap cunning and petty arts. But even if this had been otherwise, Calhoun would have had no chance whatever. It was, to say the least, exceedingly doubtful whether he could ever be elected, if nominated by the party, and therefore it was certain that he would never receive the nomination. It is true that he was not entirely without support in some of the Northern States. The Irish especially manifested everywhere some predilection for him, on account of his pedigree, and in New York, where the Whigs indulged very freely in their nativist and anti-Catholic tendencies, this predilection could almost be mistaken for genuine enthusiasm. But as the first commandment of the political decalogue of the Irish masses was to vote the regular ticket, and as his Irish extraction was nearly all they knew of him, their support was of very little avail, unless his other partisans were numerous and enthusiastic enough to scare his opponents within the party into submission. If the Southern wing unanimously and emphatically declared themselves for him, the Northern would, perhaps, not dare to resist.

But only ignorance or blind admiration could suppose for a moment that the Southern Democrats could be marched up in serried ranks to sustain his candidature. Ever since he had abjured his early national and latitudinarian bias, and become an "honest nullifier" in the service of the slavocracy, he had unfitted himself to be the leader of a great national party, because he had assumed the leadership of an extreme sectional faction. Perhaps this extreme faction was destined, in the course of time, to develop into a party which would exercise despotic sway over the whole South. Nay, it was sure to come to that, because the correct understanding of the slavery conflict must spread with its own development. As yet, however, ninety-nine out of a hundred saw the slavery question through a mist, and therefore even those who would have followed Calhoun through thick and thin, to even out-Heroding Herod, were now shocked and dismayed by his radicalism. There was probably not a single slaveholder in the whole Union who was not glad to have in the United States Senate such a champion of the peculiar institution, whose courage and will were equal to any emergency; but outside of South Carolina, the number of those who were very anxious to see him at the head of the government was comparatively small.

The Calhounites fought stubbornly and carried their point in the first preliminary question — the postponing of the national convention to the spring of 1844 — against the adherents of Van

Buren, who had wished to set it for as early a
date as November, 1843. In the other controverted previous question, however, the partisans
of Van Buren were all the more unyielding.
The Calhounites wanted the delegates to the
national convention elected by districts, while
their opponents would have the decision as to
the mode of election left to the States. If the
national convention was to represent, so far as
possible, not the political log-rollers, but the
party, the preference had undoubtedly to be
accorded to the proposition of the Calhounites;
but it was certainly somewhat strange that they,
who believed themselves to have a monopoly of
the pure states-rights doctrine, ventured to wish
to give prescriptions to the "States."

So far as their course was determined by
what they supposed to be the interest of their
respective candidates, both factions might have
saved their time and temper, and allowed this
question to take care of itself. Van Buren was
successful in the trial heat, but his final mortification was only the greater; for after all he
lost the race, although his foremost competitor
had taken the wise resolution to withdraw from
it altogether on January 20, 1844.

South Carolina was dismayed, but she did
not, as she had done heretofore, throw away her
electoral votes by voting for some candidate of

her own.   This time she submitted to the party
behest, although she did it with anything but
good grace.   The defeat of Calhoun's candidature had, however, but little to do with her anger.
She indulged once more in a spasm of loud-
mouthed passion on account of the double face
which James K. Polk, the Democratic candidate,
had seen fit to put on with regard to the tariff
question, in order to secure for himself the
electoral vote of Pennsylvania, without which
his election was deemed impossible.   Polk was
accused of having gone over, bag and baggage,
to the camp of the protectionists; indignation
meetings and dinners, with an abundance of
furious toasts, denunciations, and threats, were
the order of the day; the " Charleston Mercury "
was not satisfied with urging " legislative nullification," but invited the people of the State to
adopt " ulterior measures,'' in case that " should
prove inadequate."

There is always a fire where such volumes of
smoke becloud the sky; but this time the quantity of smoke stood in no proportion to the size
or heat of the fire.   Calhoun disapproved of
this wild ado about so little, and that now happened quite frequently which but a few weeks
before had seemed impossible, — that his name
was not mentioned at all at the political festivi-
ties of the radicals.   He did not take this slight

much to heart, nor had he any reason to do so. Not only was it a matter of course that Polk had not become a protectionist, but it was also perfectly evident that for the present the tariff was but a question of the second or third order. In both parties the opinions were far from being in full accord on this head, and in neither did the masses of those who were not most immediately interested in it feel very deeply about it. And now should a storm be artificially raised about a little more or less of duties, and thereby the gauntlet thrown into the face not only of the whole Whig party, North and South, but of all those who were too dull of comprehension to see the conservative force of nullification, and who clung to the old-fashioned idea that a law is a law, and has to be obeyed, — now, when the opportunity was offered of securing a prize of incalculable value to the democracy? Holmes and Rhett might amuse their followers by a revival of the nullification idea, "meditate ulterior measures," talk of disunion, and declare that "to this complexion it must come at last;" Calhoun had packed away his thunderbolts, and thus far he alone knew how to use them effectually.

So early as 1839 he had, in the face of almost countless declarations to the contrary, and yet apparently in good faith, astonished

the Senate by the emphatic assertion that a dissolution of the Union ever had been, and would
remain in all future time, an imaginary danger.
Replying to Mr. Buchanan, he had said: —

"The senator has done no more than justice to
that measure [the compromise tariff]. It terminated
honestly and fairly, without the sacrifice of any interest, one of the most dangerous controversies that
ever disturbed the Union or endangered its existence. Not the danger of dismemberment, as we learn
from the senator, was anticipated abroad. No, the
danger lay in a different direction. Dismemberment
is not the only mode in which our Union may be
destroyed. It is a *Federal Union*, an Union of *sovereign States*, and can be as effectually and much
more easily destroyed by *consolidation* than by *dismemberment*. He who knows anything of the history
of our race and the workings of the human breast
best understands the great and almost insuperable
difficulties in the way of dissolution. There is scarcely
an instance on record of any people, speaking the
same language and having the same government and
laws, who have ever dissolved their political connections through internal causes or struggles. . . . The
constant struggle is to enlarge, and not to divide; and
there neither is nor ever has been the least danger
that our Union would terminate in dissolution."

That was no bait thrown to "the political
sopranos" of the North. He believed what he
said, yet he did not mean to retract a single syl-

lable of what he had declared so often before.
The Union and abolition, as he had once expressed it, cannot coexist. If the spirit of the
fanatical visionaries of the North is not chained
down, then the Union is irretrievably gone, for
between the Union and slavery the South has
no choice. But he is satisfied that the South
will never be pressed before this alternative.
In the letter, before mentioned, to the citizens
of Athens, he had written : —

"Of all the questions which have been agitated
under our government, abolition is that in which we
of the South have the deepest concern. It strikes
directly and fatally, not only at our prosperity, but
our existence as a people. Should it succeed, our fate
would be worse than that of the aborigines whom we
have driven out, or the slaves whom we command.
It is a question that admits of neither concession nor
compromise. . . . There is one point in connection
with this important subject on which the South
ought to be fully informed. From all that I saw and
heard during the session, I am perfectly satisfied that
we must look to ourselves, and ourselves only, for
safety. It is perfectly idle to look to the non-slave-
holding States to arrest the attacks of the fanatics.
. . . Nor would it be less vain to look to Congress.
The same cause that prevents the non-slave-holding
States from interference in our favor at home will
equally prevent Congress. . . . But, if true to ourselves, we need neither their sympathy nor aid. The

Constitution has placed in our power ample means, *short of secession or disunion*, to protect ourselves."

We have seen more than once that he had his hours of despondency, when this conviction was severely shaken, but it was never wholly relinquished. And now he thought that the day had come when a pillar of such gigantic dimensions could be put as an additional support under the dome of slavery that it would be able to withstand all the assaults of abolitionism. The annexation of Texas was to render the Union indissoluble by strengthening the slave power so much that it would have nothing more to apprehend.

CHAPTER VIII

TEXAS

As early as May 23, 1836, Calhoun had declared in the Senate that he —

"had made up his mind not only to recognize the independence of Texas, but for her admission into this Union; and if the Texans managed their affairs prudently, they would soon be called upon to decide that question. No man could suppose for a moment that that country could ever come again under the dominion of Mexico; and he was of opinion that it was not for our interests that there should be an independent community between us and Mexico. There were powerful reasons why Texas should be a part of this Union. The Southern States, owning a slave population, were deeply interested in preventing that country from having the power to annoy them."

Thus, but one month after the battle of Jacinto, he publicly and formally announced his programme with regard to the question which was to be the pivotal point on which the fate of slavery was to turn. No other single individual did so much as he to bring about the annexation. He himself has emphatically claimed that merit, and he considered it the greatest and most beneficent achievement of his public career. Perhaps it was, as things finally turned out, but he would have cursed the day on which he put his hand to the plough, if he had known what a dragon seed was to be planted. On February 24, 1847, when the harvesting of the fatal crop had already begun, he said in the Senate : —

"I trust, Mr. President, there will be no dispute hereafter as to who is the real author of annexation. Less than twelve months since, I had many competitors for that honor: the official organ here claimed, if my memory serves me, a large share for Mr. Polk and his administration, and not less than half a dozen competitors from other quarters asserted themselves to be the real authors. But now, since the war [with Mexico] has become unpopular, they all seem to agree that I, in reality, am the author of annexation. I will not put the honor aside. I may now rightfully and indisputably claim to be the author of that great measure, — a measure which has so much extended the domains of the Union ; which has added so largely to its productive powers ; which promises so greatly to extend its commerce ; which has stimulated its industry, and given security to our most exposed frontier. I take pride to myself as being the author of this great measure."

Though there is no positive proof for it, Benton's allegation is therefore probably true, that

Calhoun was also the real author of the intrigue which was to give the annexation wheel the necessary impetus, after several years had been spent in unsuccessful attempts to put it properly into motion. Other circumstances point in the same direction, and that he at first carefully kept himself concealed in the background is satisfactorily explained by the fact that the immediate purpose of the intrigue was to bring the still enormous influence of Jackson into play.

In the beginning of 1843 a Baltimore newspaper published a letter of Gilmer, dated January 10, to " a friend " (Duff Green) in Maryland, on the necessity of the annexation of Texas. Benton says that the letter was like a flash of lightning from a clear sky. The public, however, were allowed to settle down once more into indolent unconcern, for what followed was played under cover. The letter touched most strongly the two chords which were sure to find the loudest echo in Jackson's breast: preservation against England's ambitious desires and the strengthening of the Union. But as the name of Gilmer, as well as Green, awakened the suspicion that Calhoun was seated in the prompter's box, the letter was sent to the " Sage of the Hermitage " by Aaron V. Brown, of Tennessee, who was but an unconscious tool in other hands. Jackson answered at once in the tone desired, and although the letter had been confessedly asked for only for the purpose of working on the masses, it was now carefully put away until the opportune moment for its publication should come. Those who held the wires behind the curtain had attained their immediate end. Jackson had irrevocably engaged himself for immediate annexation. Without himself being aware of it, he had thereby deprived himself of the possibility of throwing his whole weight into the scales in favor of Van Buren ; for immediate annexation was to be made the leading issue of the presidential campaign of 1844. This was another reason for the Calhounites to insist upon the postponement of the nominating convention, for they needed time to tie the South so closely down to this programme that it could not afterward draw back for the sake of a question of persons.

A few months later, one of the greatest obstacles in the way of the annexationists was removed by Webster's exit from the Cabinet. Upshur, who, after a short interregnum under Legaré, became Tyler's Secretary of State, worked with his whole energy and with considerable skill at the solution of this problem. On October 16, 1843, he proposed a treaty of annexation to the Texan agent. Texas, however,

was not now quite so eager to grasp the outstretched hand as she had been heretofore. Thanks to the efforts of England and France, there was an armistice between her and Mexico, and negotiations tending to a formal peace had been begun. Van Zandt, the Texan *chargé d'affaires* in Washington, in a letter of January 17, 1844, called the attention of Upshur to the fact that, under these circumstances, a treaty of annexation would drive Mexico to the immediate resumption of hostilities, and that it would also cost Texas the friendship of the mediating powers. He therefore confidentially inquired whether, in case the proposal of annexation were accepted by the Texan executive, the President would, even before the ratification of the treaty, protect Texas by a sufficiently strong land and maritime force against all attacks. Upshur dared not answer either yes or no. To refuse the request was to drive Texas wholly into the arms of England, while to grant it was to pledge the President to assume, on his own responsibility, as the price of Texas, the war of Texas against Mexico.

The bursting of the cannon Peacemaker on board the Princeton, on February 28, 1844, ended the embarrassment of the Secretary. To whose hands should the consummation of the annexation now be confided? The answer to

this question was not given, as one would have
expected, by the President, but by Henry A.
Wise. Already, more than two years before,
in a speech delivered in the House of Representatives, the hot-blooded Virginian had gone
into ecstasy over the idea "of planting the lone
star of the Texan banner on the Mexican capitol," of extending slavery to the Pacific, and of
robbing the Mexican churches. Now he thought
that the time had come to enter upon the realization of this sublime programme, and he was
too great a man to let the trifling considerations
of propriety, honesty, and right stand in his
way. He had the effrontery to go to McDuffie
and induce him to urge upon Calhoun the acceptance of the Secretaryship of State, causing
him (McDuffie) to believe that he (Wise) had
been sent by the President. Then he urged
Tyler to offer the place to Calhoun. The President at first declined to comply with the wish,
but he finally submitted, when he had been told
what his devoted friend had presumed to do.

Calhoun accepted, declaring at the same time
that he would resign the office so soon as annexation should become an accomplished fact.
It was the universal understanding that it was
only for this special purpose that he had been
called to the helm, and that only for this reason
he consented to become a member of the Cabinet

of the President, who had no party in Congress, and but a corporal's guard of office-holders among the people, to sustain him. He afterwards fully confirmed this view. On February 12, 1847, he said in the Senate: —

" According to my view, the time was not propitious in one respect. The then President had no party in either House. I am not certain that he had a single supporter in this, and not more than four or five in the other. It appeared to me to be a very unpropitious moment, under such circumstances, to carry through so important a measure. When it was intimated to me that I was to be nominated for the office of Secretary of State, I strongly remonstrated to my friends here; but before my remonstrance reached them, I was unanimously appointed, and was compelled to accept. I saw the administration was weak, and that the very important measure would be liable to be defeated. But circumstances made action on it inevitable."

Niles's " Register " of March 23, 1844, said:

" The nomination of John C. Calhoun to the office of Secretary of State, and the entire unanimity with which that nomination has been approved, not only by the Senate, but the public press of the country, presents the incident, in our judgment, as one of the most eventful, certainly in the life of that distinguished and talented statesman, and very possibly, also, in the future and fate of the country, the inter-

ests of which, to a vast extent, indeed, are thereby
confided to him,. at a moment of exceeding delicacy."

That the Senate unanimously confirmed the
nomination of a man of Calhoun's standing was
a matter of course; but it would have been
strange indeed if it had with entire unanimity
" approved " it, and stranger still if the whole
press, and consequently also the whole people,
had rejoiced at it, — too strange to be believed,
although some years later he himself asserted
that he had been called " by the unanimous
voice of the country to take charge of the
State Department." Just because it was in
fact "a moment of exceeding delicacy" and
"the future and the fate of the country " were,
"to a vast extent," confided to his hands, the
nomination of this most thorough-going and
most daring partisan inevitably caused the deepest concern to all the opponents of annexation,
while it gave the greatest satisfaction to all its
advocates. And he fully justified as well the
expectations of the latter as the apprehensions
of the former ; but in doing so he blurred his
fair fame. The man who had had the courage
to become " an honest nullifier " ought to have
had the courage to manage this annexation
business with perfect honesty, though with a
high hand, and not stoop to sail under false col-

ors. He would never have forgotten so far as
he did what he owed to the dignity of his country and his personal honor, if he had not thought
the annexation of such vital importance that
almost anything seemed justifiable to render
success more certain.

From the moment when Calhoun arrived in
Washington, the negotiations, which had been
rather stagnant during the interregnum, were
resumed with zeal, while public opinion was
aroused by the publication of Jackson's letter
of February 12, 1843, postdated 1844. John
Nelson, who provisionally had charge of the
State Department, had declined to accede to
the before-mentioned condition of Texas, for
the obvious reason that the President had not
the constitutional power to employ armed force
against a state with which the Union was at
peace. He had, however, assured the Texans
that Tyler was " not indisposed " to make the
desired disposition of the troops, in order that
they might be able to protect Texas at the
" proper time." Calhoun now tried his luck with
similar vague phrases, but the Texan agents
would not be paid off in such a way. On April
11 he yielded with a heavy heart, informing the
two plenipotentiaries that an order had been
issued to concentrate a powerful squadron in the
Gulf of Mexico, and " to move the disposable

forces " on the southwestern frontier " to meet
any emergency." The only object he attained
was that he was allowed to evade the greatest
difficulty by one word, which left a possibility
open to him, not, indeed, to justify the action of
the administration, but to defend it by dialectic
subtleties. He declared that, " during the pend-
ency of the treaty of annexation, the President
would deem it his duty to use all the means
placed within his power by the Constitution to
protect Texas from all foreign invasion." On
the following day the treaty was signed.

Ten days elapsed ere the treaty was submitted to the Senate. The reason of this, under
the circumstances, very surprising delay was
the wish of the Secretary to lay simultaneously
before the Senate a copy of a letter, which was
formally a reply to a dispatch of Lord Aberdeen,
and addressed to Mr. Pakenham, the English
plenipotentiary, but which, in fact, was a piece
of special pleading in justification of annexation,
directed to the people of the United States. A
more remarkable and more revolting document
has never been issued from the State Department of the country.

In the dispatch of December 26, 1843, which
had been communicated by Mr. Pakenham to
Secretary Upshur on February 26, 1844, Lord
Aberdeen had said : —

"We desire to see [slavery] abolished in Texas. With regard to the latter point, it must be and is well known, both to the United States and to the whole world, that Great Britain desires, and is constantly exerting herself to procure, the general abolition of slavery throughout the world. . . . With regard to Texas, we avow that we wish to see slavery abolished there, as elsewhere, and we would rejoice if the recognition of that country by the Mexican government should be accompanied by an engagement on the part of Texas to abolish slavery eventually, and under proper conditions, throughout the republic."

Calhoun declared in his letter of April 18, 1844, to Mr. Pakenham, that these avowals of Great Britain had made it, in the opinion of the President, "the imperious duty of the Federal government" to conclude, "in self-defence," a treaty of annexation with Texas as the most effectual measure to defeat England's intention.

"The United States have heretofore declined to meet her [Texas'] wishes; but the time has now arrived when they can no longer refuse, consistently with their own security and peace, and the sacred obligation imposed by their constitutional compact for mutual defence and protection. . . . They are without responsibility for that state of things already adverted to as the immediate cause of imposing on them, in self-defence, the obligation of adopting the

measures they have. They remained passive so long
as the policy on the part of Great Britain, which
has led to its adoption, had no immediate bearing on
their peace and safety."

It may not be correct to apply, without modi-
fication, the code of private ethics to politics;
but, however flexible political morality be, a lie
is a lie, and Calhoun knew that there was not
one particle of truth in these assertions. Almost eight years before, on May 23, 1836, as
we have seen, he himself had declared annexation to be necessary, and the first and foremost reason which he alleged for it was the
interest which the Southern States had in it,
on account of their peculiar institution. Two
years later his colleague, Mr. Preston, had
moved in the Senate, and Mr. Thompson, of
South Carolina, had also moved in the House
of Representatives, to declare annexation expedient. Several state Legislatures, as those of
Mississippi, Alabama, and Tennessee, had agitated the question with hot zeal, unreservedly
avowing that they did so "upon grounds somewhat local in their complexion, but of an import infinitely grave and interesting to the people who inhabit the southern portion of this
confederacy." In December, 1841, it was a public secret in the political circles of Washington
that Tyler had again taken up the annexation

project. It had, in fact, never been abandoned,
but only temporarily put off the order of the
day, because, for various reasons, the time had
not been deemed opportune. But on October
16, 1843, more than two months before Lord
Aberdeen's dispatch was written, and more than
four months before it was delivered, Upshur
had made the formal proposition of annexation.
Whether Calhoun had any knowledge of the
existence of this dispatch before he had consented to become the successor of Upshur we
do not know; but that he would have accepted
Tyler's invitation, and entered upon the office
with exactly the same programme, if Lord
Aberdeen's dispatch had never been written,
nobody has ever ventured to question. It is,
therefore, an incontestable fact that there was
not a particle of truth in those allegations of
the Secretary, and that he was fully conscious
of it.

To pervert the truth in such a manner required indeed a bold front. Even if the whole
world had not been familiar with the fact that
ever since the battle of San Jacinto the annexation of Texas had been but a question of time
with the whole South and the Democratic party,
Calhoun's assertion would have been simply
ridiculous. Lord Aberdeen's dispatch contained
absolutely nothing to startle or even to surprise

the United States. The avowals which, according to Calhoun, the President regarded with such "deep concern," only stated a fact as notorious as the existence of slavery itself. That England's hostility to slavery and her desire to see it everywhere abolished was "for the first time" avowed "to this government" was evidently of no consequence whatever, for it did not add a grain's weight to the importance of the fact. Lord Aberdeen expressly declared that England's policy remained unaltered, and Calhoun did not pretend to doubt in the least the truth of this assurance. The mere fact that England had seen fit to state, in an official dispatch, what every schoolboy already knew to be the case could not be a cause of alarm, and the reason which had induced her to do it was calculated to have exactly the opposite effect. Lord Aberdeen had not indulged in any threats, but the only purpose of his dispatch was to dispel any apprehensions which the United States could possibly entertain. He said : —

" We should rejoice if the recognition of that country by the Mexican government should be accompanied by an engagement on the part of Texas to abolish slavery eventually, and under proper conditions throughout the republic. But although we earnestly desire and feel it to be our duty to promote such a consummation, we shall not interfere unduly, or with

an improper assumption of authority, with either
party, in order to assure the adoption of such a course.
We shall counsel, but we shall not seek to compel or
unduly control, either party. . . . She [Great Brit-
ain] has no thought or intention of seeking to act directly or indirectly, in a political sense, on the United
States, through Texas. . . . The governments of the
slave-holding States may be assured that, although we
shall not desist from those open and honest efforts
which we have constantly made for procuring the
abolition of slavery throughout the world, we shall
neither openly nor secretly resort to any measures
which can tend to disturb their internal tranquillity,
or thereby to affect the prosperity of the American
Union."

It did not require the keen intellect of a Calhoun to see that these emphatic disclaimers
were meant to be the essential part of Lord
Aberdeen's dispatch, and not the sentences on
which he based his reply to Mr. Pakenham.
Yet it would be a great mistake to suppose that
they only served him as a pretext, because he
could find no better one, and that his uneasiness
on account of England's policy was feigned.
His alarm was not only most real, but it was
also fully justified. In the course of the negotiations with Texas, Upshur had repeatedly
avowed that the alleged ambitious designs of
Great Britain, and especially her exertions for

the abolition of slavery in the republic, imperatively demanded that the annexation should no
longer be delayed. At the same time, however,
it was acknowledged on all sides that slavery
was doomed in Texas, independently of anything England might do. Leading Texans —
e. g. Ex-President Mirabeau B. Lamar — had
frequently declared that the anti-slavery party
would soon acquire the ascendency, and that the
abolition of slavery could be effected " without
the slightest inconvenience." The most zealous
advocates of annexation in Congress had emphatically indorsed this opinion, and Upshur
himself had written to Mr. Murphy, " If Texas
should not be attached to the United States, she
cannot maintain that institution [slavery] ten
years, and probably not half that time." Calhoun held the same opinion. He informed Mr.
Pakenham that the President had " the settled
conviction that it would be difficult for Texas,
in her actual condition, to resist what she [Great
Britain] desires, *without supposing the influence
and exertions of Great Britain would be extended beyond the limits assigned by Lord Aberdeen ;* " and he added, " and this, if Texas could
not resist the consummation of the object of her
desire, would endanger both the safety and prosperity of the Union."

An independent Texas without slavery and

the permanent continuance of slavery in the Union were, however, irreconcilable. Even if this had been a mistake, as it undoubtedly was not, the opponents of the slavocracy had no reason to contest the truth of this confession, for it was the most destructive judgment which could be passed on slavery. The slavocracy declared through its most gifted representative, in an official document, that between it and liberty there existed a conflict of principle so irreconcilable, that by the simple fact of the neighborhood of independent States in which slavery did not exist, it was brought face to face with the question of life or death. Did it not follow directly from this that its political connection with free States was possible only on the supposition of the complete subservience of the latter? Was there a more forcible proof needed, or even possible, than the very demand which the slavocracy now made, in consequence of that fact? Because the slave-holding States thought their peculiar institution endangered by the existence of an independent free State, it was declared to be the "imperative duty" and a "sacred obligation" of the United States, imposed by their constitutional compact, to absorb that State into the Union, in order to prevent the abolition of slavery in it. It was not only a fact that Texas was to be annexed to make the continued exist-

ence of slavery possible there, but the fact was
officially declared before the whole world by the
executive of the Union.   The democratic republic, which had based its existence upon the rights
of man, was morally and constitutionally bound
to prevent the breaking of the chains of the
slave in a neighboring republic, though it could
be done only by adding these very chains to
those which already bound its arms.   Calhoun's
letter to Pakenham was the official proclamation
of the " nationalization " of slavery, only, however, so far as it imposed duties upon the Union,
but by no means with regard to any corresponding rights.   " With us," the Secretary declared,
the policy to be adopted in reference to the African race " is a question to be decided not by the
Federal government, but by each member of this
Union, for itself, according to its own views of
its domestic policy, and without any right on
the part of the Federal government to interfere
in any manner whatever.   Its rights and duties
are limited to protecting, under the guarantees
of the Constitution, each member of this Union
in whatever policy it may adopt in reference to
the portion within its respective limits."   The
slave-holding States had to say what was necessary to protect them in the policy they had been
pleased to adopt, and the Federal government
had to act accordingly.   The President had had

no choice. The annexation of Texas was " the most effectual, if not the only means of guarding against the threatened danger," and therefore he had acted simply " in obedience " to the constitutional obligation of the Union. In other words, it was the constitutional obligation of the Union to engage in slavery propagandism in the defence of the interests of the slavocracy, and, confessedly, even at the risk of a war; for the Secretary declared, in an official dispatch to the American representative in Mexico, that the step had been taken " in full view of all possible consequences."

If the United States had indeed assumed such sacred obligations towards the slave-holders, in establishing the Constitution, there could be no impropriety in it that Calhoun concluded his letter with a short but enthusiastic exposition of his theory of the " positive good." But what were those to think of it who did not acknowledge those obligations? Surely, the history of the United States had entered upon a new phase, if the Secretary of State could dare, in an official communication and in the name of the Federal Executive, to lecture a foreign state upon the blessings of slavery. And by his own testimony he stands convicted of having engaged in this whole correspondence partly for the very purpose of doing that, and of having

been grievously disappointed that the rejection
of the treaty prevented him from enlarging
upon this exalted theme. The "Charleston
Mercury" of November 28, 1860, published a
previously unknown letter, dated July 2, 1844,
in which Calhoun says : —

"If an opportunity should offer, I had hoped to
draw out a full correspondence by my letters to Mr.
Pakenham. They were, in part, written with that
view, and were intended to lay the foundation of a
long and full correspondence ; and I doubt not what
was intended would have been accomplished, had the
Senate done its duty [!] and ratified the treaty. Their
neglect to do so, I fear, will not only lose Texas to
the Union, but also defeat my aim in reference to
the correspondence. Had the treaty been ratified,
my last letter to Mr. Pakenham, which he transmitted to his government, would not have been left
without a reply, which would have brought on what
I intended. As it is, it will not be answered, as I
infer from Mr. Pakenham's conversation recently.
His government is content to leave to our Senate
the defence of its course, and is too wise, when it can
be avoided, to carry on a correspondence in which
they see they have little to gain. I regret it. It
will, I fear, be difficult to get another opportunity to
bring out our cause fully and favorably before the
world. I shall omit none which may afford a decent
pretext for renewing the correspondence."

Even ultra-Democratic papers and journals

in the North criticised the Pakenham letter in the severest terms. The " Democratic Review," though it advocated immediate annexation, and professed " exalted admiration, respect, and even attachment " for Calhoun, complained with bitterness that the President and his Secretary had not left a shred of the Southern doctrine, which was also that of the Northern Democrats, that slavery was a local institution, " with which the free States had nothing to do, for which they were in no wise responsible." It reproved with indignation the " volunteer discussion of the essential merits of this peculiar local institution through the peculiar organ of our collective nationality, for which, if for anything, the Union, and the whole Union, is emphatically responsible." Without reserve, it avowed that Calhoun had " nationalized " and " federalized " slavery, " actually pledging the military intervention of the country, by a simple unconstitutional executive promise, to plunge directly into war with Mexico if she should execute her threat of immediate invasion of Texas ; " and all this " on the avowed ground, the almost exclusively avowed ground, of strengthening and preserving the institution of slavery."

Such language from a leading organ of their own party might well have induced the President and his Secretary to pause and ponder.

Even if they succeeded, they were evidently playing a dangerous game. The deep-seated dissatisfaction in their own camp indicated that it would probably not be ended by their winning the stakes, and the sequel might be very far from corresponding with the beginning. But Calhoun, who so justly boasted of being wont to look to the farthest consequences of every question, had now neither ears nor eyes for anything except his immediate object. It is asserted that he obtained from Archer, of Virginia, the chairman of the Committee on Foreign Relations, the solemn promise that he would delay the Senate forty days with regard to the annexation treaty. The alleged reason for this wish was that Mexico's answer to the notification of the treaty was expected by the last day of that term. That was unquestionably an empty pretence, for in various ways this time might have easily been shortened a little ; and, besides, it had been declared from the first that Mexico would not be allowed to interfere in any way whatever in this question. The term was evidently fixed with relation to the national convention of the Democratic party, which was to meet two days earlier at Baltimore. Calhoun wanted to make sure of the party with regard to the main question, ere he allowed the Senate to come to a decision on the treaty. The " Spectator," the reputed organ of Calhoun in Washington, had formally declared that Van Buren was to be considered " as beside the presidential canvass," because he had refused to pledge himself for immediate annexation. Therewith the programme was announced which the annexationists were resolved to impose upon the convention at all hazards. After a long and arduous struggle over the preliminary questions, they triumphed completely. The majority vote which Van Buren received at the first ballot was a bootless compliment. His partisans knew that they had lost the game before the voting commenced. On the eighth ballot the name of Governor Polk, of Tennessee, appeared for the first time, and on the next ballot he was nominated. Polk was what, in the political slang of to-day, is called " a dark horse ; " but as to the test question, he could have been implicitly trusted, even if the platform had not pledged the party to " the re-annexation of Texas at the earliest practicable period."

The impatience which Calhoun had betrayed in the first stages of his annexation campaign proved that he would have manœuvred with more quickness and boldness if he had not had good reason to apprehend that the Senate would take serious objection to his policy. It was well known that the treaty would not be supported

by all those who were in favor of speedy annexation. The Pakenham correspondence was a
two-edged sword. Calhoun had cut himself as
badly as he had cut his opponents. He had
succeeded in consolidating the South to the extent that he had expected; but, at the same
time, he had aroused the feeling of the North
to such a degree that even the best disposed
senators were afraid that they would commit
political suicide by voting for this treaty, after
it had been officially based on such grounds.
Besides, they did not see why such immoderate
haste should be necessary. Tyler's and Calhoun's interests might be well enough served
by it, but that was only another reason for them
to curb the over-zealous administration. While
there were but few, if any, senators who, under
any circumstances, would have been anxious to
smooth the way of either the President or the
Secretary in the pursuit of any personal ends,
the majority deemed it a duty to administer to
them a severe rebuke for their gross infringe-
ments upon the rights of Congress and the lack
of consideration for the Senate, which had characterized the whole transaction. Even zealous
annexationists indulged in searching and caus-
tic criticisms of the treaty and all the attendant
circumstances, and on June 8 it was rejected by
a vote of thirty-five against sixteen.

The dismay of Tyler and Calhoun was great, but they were not in the least daunted. They were bent upon attaining their end. If it was not to be secured in this way, nothing was to deter them from trying any other which promised success, though they might have to ride rough-shod over the Constitution and all the constitutional doctrines which they had heretofore professed. On the second day after the rejection of the treaty, the President sent a message to the House of Representatives, accompanied by all the documents relating to the question. The essence of the message was contained in the declaration that Congress was "fully competent, in some other form of proceeding, to accomplish everything that a formal ratification of the treaty could have accomplished." That was in fact an appeal from the Senate, which had the unquestionable right to reject a treaty, to the House of Representatives, to which no power has been given by the Constitution in relation to treaties. What was the sense of rendering the consent of two thirds of the Senate indispensable for the conclusion of every treaty, if, after a treaty had been rejected by the Senate, a simple majority of both Houses of Congress had the right ·virtually to ratify it, by accomplishing in some other form what the treaty was to have accomplished? Like a

French cavalier of the old régime, Tyler waived
away this question with the bold reply, " The
great question is, not as to the manner in which
it shall be done, but whether it shall be accomplished or not." That such an answer would
not have been given, unless it was fully approved by Calhoun, will not be doubted. But
when had the most reckless Federalists ever
dared to profess such an unblushing latitudina-
rianism, or to nationalize the Union to such an
extent by pushing the Constitution aside, and
giving the Federal government *carte blanche* in
a question more important than any other ever
submitted to it? Verily, the country had fallen
upon strange times, if such a doctrine could be
officially proclaimed by the President, under the
sanction of the man who had come very near
plunging the Union into a civil war, by pushing
his states-rights theory to such extremities that
he found, in the right of nullification, the main-
stay of the Union and its great conservative
principle.

The President had made no definite proposition to Congress, but the language of the message of June 10 was too plain to admit any
doubt that the administration would not let
matters quietly take their own course after the
close of the session. The check which it had
received had made it only more determined and

bolder. Upon a notification from the Texan
Secretary of State that Mexico intended a new
invasion, Calhoun stated that his letter of April
11 had promised armed intervention only in
case this emergency should occur while the
treaty of annexation was pending. We have
seen how loath he had been to give this promise,
which his immediate predecessor, Nelson, had
declared unconstitutional, and yet he now, September 10, after the treaty had been rejected,
volunteered to extend the obligation to the whole
time during which "the *question* of annexation" should remain "pending." In a formal
and constitutional sense, however, annexation
was not now at all a pending question. That
the President had expressed the wish to see it
ultimately accomplished, no matter in what
way, and that some members of Congress had
suggested this and that, did not and could not
make it a *question* in this sense. The treaty
had been rejected, the Executive had not entered upon new negotiations with Texas for another treaty, and Congress was not even in session. The annexation of Texas was, therefore,
no more a "pending question" than the tariff,
the bank, or any other political problem in
which the people took a lively interest. There
was absolutely nothing to be found in the actual condition of things from which even the

most subtle dialectics could deduce any international rights or obligations. Besides, the Senate had given it to be understood, in no very ambiguous manner, that, at least in what concerned the President's independent initiative, it did not approve of the promises made in the letter of April 11. Calhoun, therefore, forbore to announce, in express words, an armed intervention; but the declaration that the United States would feel themselves " highly offended " by a renewal of the war, and that they would not " permit it," virtually amounted to the same thing. When the news came that Mexican agents were agitating the Indians at the frontier, — news which never failed to reach Washington, whenever it was opportune that it should come, — Calhoun followed up his protest of September 10 by authorizing (September 17) the Union troops to enter Texas as soon as the Texans should desire it.

In their hot pursuit of the long-coveted prize, which had so unexpectedly slipped through their fingers, Tyler and Calhoun were, in fact, as ready " to assume the full responsibility " for any step which promised to bring them nearer the goal as Andrew Jackson had ever been when the constitutionality or legality of his acts was called into question. Perhaps they would have proceeded with a little more caution, if the

Southern annexationists had not set them the
example of an unblushing recklessness, which
was without a parallel in the whole history of
the Union. The threats of disunion, if the
North dared to resist this extension of the domain of slavery, were too common to make the
desired impression. Much more effect had the
announcement that the North would have to
choose between Texas and the abolition of the
tariff of 1842. There were many respectable
men in the North who honestly believed slavery
to be a sin and a curse, but who loved their
pockets more than they hated slavery. With
others, again, their party attachment was
stronger than their hatred and fear of slavery.
They benumbed their consciences with the illusion that they could cleanse their skirts of all
responsibility by protesting against the annexation and recommending the election of anti-an-
nexationists to Congress, while they voted for
Polk. As to the office-seekers, a slight raising
of the party whip was, of course, sufficient to
make them all zealous annexationists, no matter
what their convictions had been before the Baltimore Convention; their convictions had to be
stored away for the time being, for it would
have been foolhardiness to carry such heavy baggage in so hot a race, with so many competitors.
So the annexationists could count upon the

whole Democratic party of the North, though
a considerable part of it either entirely disapproved of annexation, or, at least, thought immediate annexation inexpedient. Yet, in spite
of that and of their complete control over the
Federal patronage, the annexationists would have
lost the election, if the Liberty Party, instead
of putting up a candidate of their own, had supported the Whigs, in order to bar the way to
the former. The votes of that party caused
the Whigs to lose the States of New York and
Michigan, and with them the election. Polk
was elected, but the history of the election
proved beyond contradiction that the majority
of the people were opposed to immediate annexation. Tyler's annual message of December 3,
however, not only asserted the contrary, but declared that both Houses of Congress had been
instructed, — by "a controlling majority of the
people, and a large majority of the States," —
"in terms the most emphatic," to accomplish
annexation immediately, and he therefore recommended it to be done in the most simple way,
namely, by joint resolution.

How often had the holy anger of Calhoun's
constitutional and political conscience been
aroused by Jackson's daring to put such inter-
pretations upon elections! Yet everything with
which Jackson could be justly reproached in

this respect was mere child's play, in comparison with the monstrosity of the political heresy of this assertion and with its brazen disregard of truth; and that Tyler neither would nor could have ventured to make it without Calhoun's consent nobody will contest. It was simply not true that the election had presented to the people for its decision "the isolated question of annexation." If it had been true, the result could, perhaps, by means of Benton's "*demos krateo*" principle, have been tortured into an instruction "to both branches of Congress, by their respective constituents;" but neither the most searching chemical analysis nor the most powerful microscope could discover the slightest vestige of *this* "*demos krateo* principle" in the *Constitution*. Besides, the theory of the message refuted itself in such a way that not another word is needed to show it up as a political counterfeit of the most bungling kind. If the electoral votes of the several States were binding instructions to the respective senators, the eleven States which had voted for Clay had instructed their senators, "in terms the most emphatic," against annexation. The Union, however, consisted at the time of but twenty-six States, and the least important of treaties required the assent of two thirds of the senators. Thus the "instruc-

tions" which the senators had received from
the "States" made it impossible to accomplish
annexation in the way which Tyler himself had
acknowledged to be at least "the most suitable."
Yet the "instructions" from a simple majority
of States would, by the theory advanced, have
made it the imperative duty of the Senate to
conclude, without any further previous consideration, a compact with a foreign power, than
which it is impossible to imagine one more important. If the "people," by means of a presidential election, could oblige Congress to incorporate a foreign state, and if Congress could
effect such incorporation by a simple majority
resolution, the "consolidation" of the Union
was complete, and its confederate character was
completely and forever lost. The theory of the
message was, in fact, the subversion of all the
underlying principles of Calhoun's political doctrines, upon which he had based his defence of
the "peculiar institution." In spite of that,
however, he consented to this theory without
any compunction, because the slavocracy would
have to die, and to die beyond resurrection, if it
could not get more land and create more slave-
holding States.

Congress did not accede to the proposition of
the President without a little more ado. The
House of Representatives, indeed, was satisfied

John Tyler

with having the line of the Missouri Compromise continued through Texas; but, in the Senate, a back door had to be provided for the consciences of those annexationists who held that the only constitutional way of effecting the annexation was by treaty. The resolution of the House of Representatives was amended, by authorizing the President to negotiate another treaty of annexation, if he should deem it more advisable to do so than to submit the joint resolution to Texas. Benton and the other senators, who had sustained the above-mentioned constitutional view, never deigned to inform the people whence they derived the right to give the President the choice to bring about the annexation, either in the constitutional or in an unconstitutional way, as he should think best. The crutch with which they limped over this obstacle was McDuffie's declaration that Calhoun would not have the " audacity " to choose the unconstitutional way, and submit the joint resolution to Texas. Did they really so little know the man who had dared to become " an honest nullifier " ? On March 1, 1845, the joint resolution was approved by the President. On Calhoun's advice " to act without delay," the Cabinet were summoned the next day, and concurred in the opinion of the Secretary of State, who wrote his dispatch, inviting Texas to accept the terms of the joint resolution, the same night, and sent it off " late in the evening of March 3," a few hours before the expiration of Tyler's term of office. His reasons for acting thus he has repeatedly stated with a candor which proves that he would have been equal to a much greater " audacity," if it had been necessary to secure his object. In the dispatch to Mr. Donelson he wrote, " But the decisive objection to the amendment of the Senate is that it would endanger the ultimate success of the measure. . . . A treaty . . . must be submitted to the Senate for its approval, and run the hazard of receiving the votes of two thirds of the members present; which could hardly be expected, if we are to judge from recent experience." And on February 24, 1847, he declared in the Senate, " I selected the resolution of the House in preference to the amendment of which the senator from Missouri was the author, . . . because I clearly saw, not only that it was every way preferable, but the only certain mode by which annexation could be effected. . . . That the course I adopted did secure the annexation, and that it was indispensable for that purpose, I have high authority in my possession."

Thus it was that he triumphed over all obstacles, and succeeded in virtually accomplishing the purpose for which he had consented to

become a member of Tyler's Cabinet. What
right had he to complain that the work was
continued by his successors in the spirit in
which it had been begun by him? Why should
Polk's diplomatic conscience be more conform-
able to the code of private morals than his
own? In order to get Texas, he, the sternest
and most jealous partisan of strict construction,
had loosened the bridle of the Constitution more
than any of his predecessors had ever dared to
do. What right had he to cry out and wash
his hands of all responsibility, when his disciples refused to listen to his warning voice, and
rushed on in mad zeal along the track upon
which he had started them? He had hit the
mark, but the ball pierced the target and continued its fatal flight.

Calhoun's friends expected that he would be
called upon to finish the great work which he
had directed with so much skill and energy,
and it is asserted that he shared their opinion.
We cannot prove the contrary, but are inclined
to think that he judged Polk more correctly.
If he really expected to remain at the head of
the Cabinet, the wish was father to the thought.
Polk certainly never intended to tender him the
office. Now, after the annexation of Texas was
as good as accomplished, the whole party would
probably have been rather dissatisfied to see the

first place awarded to the leader of the small
faction on its extreme left wing, which was so
easily tempted to break through the bonds of
party discipline and assume an independent
position. Especially Jackson would have been
deeply mortified, and Polk, who would never
have reached the top of the ladder if he had not
clung so faithfully to the heels of the general,
was not inclined to array Jackson's still enormous influence against the administration. Besides, it was asserted that the offended politicians of New York had exacted the promise that,
in consideration of their supporting the nominees
of the Baltimore Convention, Calhoun should be
discarded. But, above all, Polk was personally
not at all desirous to put a political star of
this magnitude and brilliancy in too close prox-
imity with the rushlight of his own talents and
achievements. Calhoun's character and whole
political course absolutely forbade his honest
subordination under another man's mind and
will, and Polk was too ambitious and self-con-
scious to be a mere figure-head where it was his
right and even his duty to be the real chief.
On the other hand, he was well aware that
openly to slight the Calhounites in the person
of their leader would be the extreme of folly.
He therefore offered him the first diplomatic
office, the legation at the Court of St. James,

undoubtedly fully satisfied that the honor would be politely declined.

Many years before, at the end of 1819, when Mr. Gallatin had expressed the wish to be recalled from Paris, Adams had asked Calhoun whether he would accept the post. Calhoun had then answered " that he was well aware that a long and familiar practical acquaintance with Europe was indispensable to complete the education of an American statesman, and regretted that his fortune would not bear the cost of it." Calhoun devoted much time to the management of his estate, and he had the reputation of being an uncommonly experienced and efficient planter; but his pecuniary circumstances remained modest, though he lived with his numerous family in unostentatious but solid comfort, and could indulge in the true luxury of always bidding a hearty welcome to the throngs of friends who came to enjoy the hospitality of his table and the pleasure of his genial company. It is, therefore, very possible that he would have declined, under all circumstances, Polk's offer, for the same reason which had dictated his answer to the overtures of Adams. But it is unquestionable that he would have taken the same course for political reasons, if he had been the wealthiest man on the continent. Polk knew perfectly well that he paid Calhoun an

empty compliment, for it was certain that his
going to London in such critical times would
be considered by himself and by his political
friends a kind of desertion. It was too late in
the day to go to Europe in order to finish his
education as a statesman. If he now accepted
a diplomatic post, it could only be for one of
two reasons: either because he wanted to gratify his ambition and vanity, or because he
thought that he could render his country important services. This kind of ambition, however, though its fire had not entirely ceased
to burn in his bosom, was no longer strong
enough to determine his resolution in a question
of such moment; and though it might soon become of great consequence who was the representative of the United States in London, yet
he could evidently do much more to avert any
dangers which might possibly arise if he should
stay in his old place in the Senate, where he
was not obliged to follow the instructions of
other people, but was entirely free to be guided
by his own opinion. His character and the
peculiar part which he had played these last
fifteen years in the history of the Union absolutely forbade his being an instrument in other
men's hands; either he had to direct the policy
of the Union, so far as that could be done by
the Executive, or he had to remain the inde-

pendent senator, the foremost champion of the
slavocracy and the leader of the ultra states-
rights faction. The former he could not do,
and weighty reasons demanded that he should
once more return to the post which he had occupied so long with so much distinction. Un-
hesitatingly he had thrown his influence into
the scales for Polk, because he had only to
choose between him and Clay; but the late Governor of Tennessee and Speaker of the House
of Representatives would not have been his own
first choice, and he was far from being satisfied
that either the foreign or domestic policy of the
new President would entirely accord with his
own views. The wild denunciations in which
the radicals of South Carolina had indulged
during the campaign had been disapproved by
him, but he thought it wise not only to wait,
but also to watch. He therefore readily returned to his seat in the Senate, which was
vacated by his successor as a matter of course.
His position in his State was such that he might
consider the seat as belonging to him of right,
so long as he was willing to remain in public
life.

CHAPTER IX

OREGON AND THE MEXICAN WAR

WHEN Calhoun was invited to become the head of Tyler's Cabinet, the "Richmond Enquirer" said, "We cannot entertain a moment's doubt that he has been selected with a special regard to the question of Oregon and the annexation of Texas." The order of the two matters ought to have been reversed, but it was correct that, next to Texas, Oregon was the most important subject in the order of the day, and that it required a master's hand to bring the negotiations with England to a mutually satisfactory termination. Yet it is very unlikely that Calhoun himself harbored the delusion that he would add a new laurel leaf to his wreath by accomplishing that task. Everything that could be said in support of the claims of the United States he counted up with his customary ability, but he had no new fact and no new argument to add to what had been repeated already a dozen times. He, therefore, made no more impression upon Pakenham than Pakenham made upon him by reiterating for the tenth time what England had to say in support of her claims. In this way it was evidently impossible to advance a single inch on either side. The two powers could go on telling their respective stories to the end of days, and the only result of it would be the heaping of proof upon proof that nothing could be thus attained. The journals of the discoverers and the legal arguments were certainly of some weight, and an impartial examination of them undoubtedly leads to the conclusion that of the two incomplete and contestable titles that of the United States was the better. But no log-books and no principles of public and international law, as laid down by Hugo Grotius, could avail anything against the simple fact that, by a solemn and repeatedly renewed agreement, the Territory was held in joint occupancy by the two powers, and that the possession of it was deemed by both an interest of such moment that neither would ever voluntarily yield the whole ground to the other. As neither wished to continue the *status quo*, and still less to cut the knot with the sword, a compromise was the only way to settle the controversy. Great Britain therefore proposed to submit it to an arbitrator; but on January 21, 1845, Calhoun, in the name of the President, declined this offer, upon the ground that "it would be unadvisable to enter-

tain a proposal to resort to any other mode, so
long as there is hope of arriving at a satisfactory settlement by negotiation."

There the matter was allowed to rest for the
time. Tyler and Calhoun left it to their successors exactly as they had found it. Yet it is
to be supposed that Calhoun was tolerably well
satisfied, and thought that he had done the best
thing possible, under the circumstances, for the
interest of the United States. In the beginning
of 1843 a bill for the occupation and settlement of the Oregon Territory had been before
Congress. Calhoun opposed its passage, because he thought that the United States had no
right, under the convention of 1818–27, to offer
land bounties to settlers. With many others,
he apprehended that this might lead to a breach
with England, and he deprecated it as the greatest folly on the part of the United States to do
anything tending to provoke a decision by arbitrament of arms. In six weeks England could
bring a strong naval and military force from
China to the mouth of the Columbia River,
while the American fleet, which would have to
double Cape Horn, would need about six months
to reach that point; and the overland march
from Missouri would require at least one hundred and twenty days, if indeed it were possible
to sustain any considerable force in a region so

destitute of supplies. The United States would, therefore, surely be worsted in a conflict of arms for the dominion over that distant country. On the other hand, the almost miraculous growth of the population of the United States and the impetus with which it was " rolling towards the shores of the Pacific " rendered it an absolute certainty that, in a comparatively short time, the United States would be as much stronger in Oregon than England as England was now stronger than they. Therefore Calhoun's advice was, " Let us be wise and abide our time ; it will accomplish all that we desire with more certainty and with infinitely less sacrifice than we can without it." " All we want, to effect our object in this case, is ' a wise and masterly inactivity.' "

Calhoun had now acted in strict conformity to this programme, and, as a settlement of the controversy according to the wishes of the United States was as yet impossible, it is to be presumed that he was not exactly dissatisfied that the negotiation had had no result except to add another bundle of useless papers to the archives of the State Department.

President Polk's inaugural address made a sharp cut through this policy of " wise and masterly inactivity " by declaring the title of the United States to the Territory " clear and

unquestionable." The whole country was thrown
into wild excitement by this declaration, for if
Congress took the same view of the question
the breach with England seemed almost inevitable. That the President, in spite of his
" blustering announcement," as Lord John Rus-
sell called that declaration, addressed a compromise proposition to England was a surprise;
but the chances of an amicable settlement were
not thereby increased, for in one of the earlier
negotiations the United States had been willing to yield more than what was now offered
by Polk. Since England had then rejected
the greater concession as insufficient, it was a
matter of course that she would not now accept
the smaller offer. Besides, Polk had accompanied it with the declaration that " he would
not have consented to yield any portion of the
Oregon Territory had he not found himself
embarrassed, if not committed, by the acts of his
predecessors." He therefore withdrew his offer
after it had been rejected by England, and his
annual message declared " that no compromise
which the United States ought to accept can be
effected." At the same time he advised the
abrogation of the convention of 1818–27. The
consequence was that, as Calhoun afterwards
stated, " stocks of every description fell, marine
insurances rose, commercial pursuits were sus-

pended, and our vessels remained inactive at the wharves." General Cass, after previous consultation with the President and Secretary of State, poured oil into the flames by a violent speech (December 15, 1845), which culminated in the assertion that " war is almost upon us." Several senators expressed in strong terms their dissatisfaction with the course which the influential senator from Michigan had seen fit to pursue. It seemed, however, as if the majority of both Houses of Congress would only too willingly follow the lead of the administration. On December 18, Senator Allen, the chairman of the Committee on Foreign Relations, moved a joint resolution, advising the President " to give, forthwith, notice to Great Britain that the government of the United States . . . will terminate the convention existing relative to the joint occupancy of the Oregon Territory." And on January 5, 1846, the Committee on Foreign Relations of the House moved a resolution, peremptorily demanding " that the President of the United States forthwith cause notice to be given to the government of Great Britain," etc.

The right to give notice at any time they pleased had been expressly stipulated by the high contracting powers in the convention of 1827. The adoption of those resolutions, there-

fore, would not have given Great Britain any
just cause of complaint. The spirit, however,
which actuated the hotspurs made the words
almost equivalent to a declaration of war. The
notice that the United States wanted the joint
occupancy to terminate was understood to be
a notification that Great Britain must abandon
her claims at once and absolutely, or take the
consequences. " Fifty-four forty or fight " was
the plain language of the radicals. A set of
resolutions, introduced by Senator Hannegan,
boldly denied even the power of the government to settle the controversy by any compromise or to concede one foot of the Territory to
England. Calhoun, on December 30, 1845, introduced a set of counter-resolutions, asserting
the power of the government which Hannegan
denied; stating the fact that, however clear the
title of the United States to the whole Territory
might be in their opinion, there were conflicting claims to the possession of the same between them and Great Britain; and declaring
that the President, in proposing the forty-ninth
degree as a compromise boundary, did not
" abandon the honor, the character, or the best
interests of the American people."

These counter-resolutions rolled a heavy load
from the breasts of all those in whose opinion
it was a criminal folly to treat this question in

a manner which, if it was not intended to provoke a war, actually pressed the British lion to the alternative of crouching like a whipped spaniel, or of using his powerful claws. It was generally believed that it depended upon Calhoun whether passion and ambition or cool statesmanship should rule the day, and though the resolutions were clad in a strictly negative form they left no doubt which side could count upon his determined support.

To-day, probably, nobody will contest that this is one of his best claims upon the gratitude of his country, and yet it cannot be denied that there was a good deal of solid matter in the avalanche of bitter complaints and stinging reproaches which the Northwestern radicals hurled against him and all the Democrats of the South. Calhoun had carefully abstained from laying down any positive programme in his resolutions, because his programme was now, as it had been in 1843, to have none, — the policy of "wise and masterly inactivity." And the reasons which he had then adduced for this course were now as good as they had been at that time. He was probably right in supposing that a war would result in the loss of " every inch " of the Territory; nor could anybody question that time was the ally of the United States, and was working in their favor

with a force which Great Britain would ultimately be unable to resist. But this being so,
why did he not pursue his reasoning to the last
consequences? According to his argument, the
United States were sure to get the whole Territory, if they would but have patience and bide
their time ; yet he did not contend for the continuation of the joint occupancy so long as
England could be prevailed upon not to give
notice. He still asserted that, in his opinion,
the title of the United States to the whole Territory was good, and that he wished to secure
the possession of the whole to them ; but the
whole tenor of his resolutions, and especially
the last one, which declared that the offer of
the forty-ninth degree was not an abandonment of their " best interests," clearly indicated
that a fair compromise would meet with his
approval.

That was the wisest and therefore a truly
patriotic policy, but would he have advocated
it if Oregon had been situated south of Mason and Dixon's line? The history of the
annexation of Texas answers this question in
an unmistakable manner. Only party passion
could doubt that the patriotism of the South
was strong enough to defend with energy the
rights of the Union, whenever these rights were
really " clear and unquestionable." But it is

equally certain that Calhoun and the other representatives of the South were not at all anxious to assume any burdens and submit to any
sacrifices in the defence of questionable rights,
if the North was to have the benefit of them.
As in the opinion of Giddings, the indomitable
enemy of slavery, the necessity to restore the
equilibrium between the two sections, which
had been disturbed by the annexation of Texas
in favor of the South, imperatively demanded
that the United States should maintain their
claims to Oregon at every hazard, so the South
apprehended that this equilibrium would be
disturbed in favor of the North by securing the
whole Territory to the Union, and therefore
was determined not to go a hair's breadth beyond what the honor of the republic really required. Calhoun had openly avowed that, so
far as it depended upon him, the annexation of
Texas should be effected without delay, though
it should lead to a war, in which England might
be found on the side of Mexico. With regard
to the Oregon question, however, he was sure
to oppose with the utmost energy any policy
tending to endanger the peace of the Union,
and the more energetically, the more that policy
was likely to result in an extension of the
Union territory in the north. For a war with
Great Britain would be, under all circumstances,

most detrimental to the interests of the South,
and might easily put the very existence of slavery into imminent danger. In and out of Congress, leading men of the South openly avowed
that these considerations for the special interests of their section determined their course,
and there was in fact no reason to conceal the
truth. If the policy of the radicals was sure to
do much harm to the South, and if it was, to
say the least, very doubtful whether the United
States as a whole would derive any benefit from
it, the adoption of it would have been not only
an act of folly, but a wrong on the part of the
North. But, however sound the arguments of
Calhoun and the other representatives of the
South were, their sayings and doings, now that
an interest of the North was at stake, did not
agree with what they had said and done when
they had contended for the interests of their
"peculiar institution." The difference was the
less justifiable because then the United States
had had to deal with a *political* problem, while
they had now to maintain, as they contended,
an existing *right*. Besides, the South stood
"pledged," as Bedinger, of Virginia, admitted,
to support the policy of the West with regard
to Oregon, in consideration of what the West
had done for the South with regard to Texas.
It is true, Calhoun had been personally no

party to this bargain, which had been concluded and solemnly proclaimed to the whole world by the Baltimore Convention. The charge of "Punic faith," which Hannegan hurled against the South, was therefore too strong a term, so far as he was concerned. But he had not uttered a single syllable against this bargain, and the West had a right to infer from his silence that he approved and sanctioned it as well as the rest of the Baltimore platform. As he was the foremost leader of the annexationists, perfect candor would have required a declaration that he personally intended to stick to his policy of "masterly inactivity;" and now he even abandoned that, and declared himself in favor of a compromise. Public opinion and history have decided the controversy in favor of this policy. No blame rests upon Calhoun for what he did now. His annexation game had not been played entirely above board, and for this wrong he had now to pay the just penalty. What he had done then exposed him now to the charges of inconsistency and bad faith. And that was but the first drop of the bitter cup, which his own hand had pressed to his lips by the deed concerning which he declared to the last, "To no act of my life do I revert with more satisfaction."

On January 17, 1846, Webster had written to Mr. Sears, "Most of the Whigs in the Sen-

ate incline to remain rather quiet, and to follow
the lead of Mr. Calhoun. He is at the head
of a party of six or seven, and as he professes
still to be an administration man it is best to
leave the work in his hands, at least for the
present." Seward was very indignant at this
" ill-starred coalition of nullifiers with Whigs,
to save slavery and free trade." Webster,
however, was certainly right in believing that
the surest way to check the wild policy of the
Western radicals effectually and in time was to
confide the lead of the opposition to a professed
" administration man ; " and Seward labored
under a great mistake in supposing that he
and the Western radicals were fighting at the
side of the administration, against this opposition, by contending in full earnest for the
extreme views of President Polk's messages.
Calhoun and his followers and allies would
probably have succeeded in enlisting public
opinion as strongly in favor of a sensible and
sober policy, even if Polk had really wished to
see the uncompromising course, which he officially advocated, adopted by Congress. But
their task was undoubtedly rendered much easier by the fact that the President was secretly
as anxious as they to see the fire quenched,
which he had stirred up into so dangerous a
conflagration. As to this question, Calhoun was

a much better administration man than he was himself aware of. But in serving the President here, where he apparently crossed the policy of the administration, he also unwittingly promoted its ultimate designs, which filled his mind with the greatest apprehensions for the future of the country.

On March 16, 1846, Calhoun had said in the Senate, "A further inducement for dispatch in settling the Oregon question is that upon it depends the settlement of the question with Mexico." In this Polk perfectly agreed with him. Their ways parted only when they came to the question how and under what conditions the settlement with Mexico was to be effected. One of the main reasons why Calhoun so earnestly strove to bring about a compromise with England was the delusion that this was the surest way to avert a war with Mexico, while, in fact, the apprehension of a war with England was the only thing which, perhaps, could have deterred Polk from his aggressive policy towards Mexico. No more unjust accusation could be brought against Polk than that he wished a war with Mexico. He and his Cabinet infinitely preferred the crooked ways of diplomacy to a war even with an enemy so weak that they could afford to despise him. They only were irrevocably determined to obtain from Mexico what

they could not get without a war, and thus it
became a "necessity" to "compel" Mexico,
just as Calhoun had been "compelled" to accept the office of Secretary of State, because the
annexation of Texas was a "necessity."

Calhoun had accompanied to the Mexican
government the notification of the treaty of annexation with the assurance "that it is his [the
President's] desire to settle all questions between the two countries which may grow out of
this treaty, or any other cause, on the most liberal and satisfactory terms, including that of
boundary." On March 31, 1845, his declaration
was repeated almost literally by Mr. Shannon
on behalf of President Polk. Calhoun, however, had intended to negotiate honestly with
Mexico about the contested boundary of Texas,
while, according to Polk, "the most liberal and
satisfactory terms" were, that not a single inch
of the territory claimed by Texas could, under
any circumstances, be granted to Mexico, and
that, in order to prevent future conflicts, New
Mexico and California should be sold by Mexico to the United States. As Mexico could not
be prevailed upon to see the question in the
same light, the American army, under General
Taylor, was ordered (January 13, 1846) to take
possession of the contested strip of land, and to
assume such an attitude that an appeal to the

arbitrament of the sword was inevitable, unless Mexico had entirely lost her self-respect.

Calhoun heard of the fatal order only " a long time after " it had been given. He deprecated it, because he clearly foresaw its pernicious consequences, and wished the Senate to take some action forcing the President to recall it. But he himself refused to move in the matter, because, as he said, " it was important I should maintain the kindest and most friendly relations, in order that I should have some weight in bringing the Oregon question to an amicable settlement." That this was no afterthought is fully proved by his whole subsequent course with regard to the Mexican war. But it is equally certain that Calhoun here committed the greatest and most fatal political blunder of his whole career. Polk knew as well and better than he that Taylor's advance from Corpus Christi would lead to a war with Mexico, and it was folly to think it possible that a President of the United States could see a double war with Mexico and Great Britain in the same light as it would be seen by a demagogical stump-speaker, intoxicated by his own spread-eagle harangues. The order of January 13, 1846, would never have been issued if Polk had not made up his mind to satisfy England with regard to Oregon. Calhoun could have crossed

the way of the President in the most determined
manner, without risking anything except his
standing as an " administration man," and that
he was sure to lose at any rate.

On Saturday, May 9, 1846, Polk received the
welcome news that a skirmish had taken place
on the eastern bank of the Rio Grande. On
the following Monday he sent a message to Congress, which culminated in the assertion that
" war exists, and, notwithstanding all our efforts
to avoid it, exists by the act of Mexico herself."
The House of Representatives at once indorsed
the bold statement, without any examination
of its truth, and without allowing the minority
a single minute to develop their views of the
question.   In the Senate a short debate could
not be avoided, but here, too, the administration
party succeeded in preventing the minority from
entering at all upon a previous examination of
the main question.   Calhoun demanded in vain
" at least one day " to consult the documents
accompanying the message, " as containing the
ground on which the bill [" for the prosecution
of the existing war "] was to pass."   In vain
did he and those who acted with him repeatedly
express their willingness to vote at once " the
amount of supplies contained in the bill, or even
a greater amount," so that the succoring of
Taylor might not be delayed one hour, in case

he should really stand in need of it. In vain did
Calhoun demonstrate that hostilities did not necessarily constitute a war, and that the President's
assertion was not and could not be true, because
the right to declare war was granted by the
Constitution exclusively to Congress. In vain
was attention called to the fact that it was not
known as yet whether the Mexican government would approve of General Arista's cross-
ing the Rio Grande. In vain was the majority
reminded that the history of the United States
afforded more than one example of most outrageous hostilities, in which they had been the
assailed party, and which yet had not led to a
war, and much less had anybody ventured to
assert that these in themselves constituted a
war. Like the President, the majority wanted
the war in order to conquer New Mexico and
California, and therefore no reasons, however
weighty and unanswerable, could be of any
avail. On May 13 the war bill was passed by
a vote of forty against two. Calhoun had abstained from voting, for " he could neither vote
affirmatively nor negatively," because " he had
no certain evidence to go on." " He could not
agree to make war on Mexico by making war
on the Constitution." Therewith he ceased to
be an " administration man," without joining
the opposition. More solitary than ever before,

he pursued his independent course. He neither broke nor bent, but the furrows on his forehead deepened, and his eyes looked more gloomy and careworn than ever; for without abandoning a single delusion as to the nature or future of slavery, he saw but too clearly that the more successfully the war was waged, the more the "peculiar institution" and, in consequence, the existence of the Union, became endangered.

Two presidential messages — one of August 4, 1846, addressed to the Senate, and the other of the 8th of the same month, addressed to Congress — indirectly avowed the real purposes of the war, which everybody had known from the first. Polk asked two million dollars to negotiate a peace, in which he proposed to pay "a fair equivalent" for some territory which Mexico was to cede, in order to adjust the boundary by a line "securing perpetual peace and good neighborhood between the two republics." The House promptly acted on the suggestion of the President, but on motion of Mr. Wilmot, of Pennsylvania, a proviso was attached, by which slavery and involuntary servitude were forever prohibited in any territory which might be acquired from Mexico. An amendment, moved by Mr. Wick, of Iowa, which divided the eventual acquisitions by the line of the Missouri Compromise, was rejected by a vote of 69 against

54. The fulfilment of the dark forebodings which had caused Calhoun to oppose the war with all his energy had therewith begun. On February 24, 1847, he said in the Senate : —

"Every senator knows that I was opposed to the war; but none save myself knows the depth of that opposition. With my conceptions of its character and consequences, it was impossible for me to vote for it. When, accordingly, I was deserted by every friend on this side of the House, including my then honorable colleague among the rest [Mr. McDuffie], I was not shaken in the least degree in reference to my course. On the passage of the act recognizing the war, I said to many of my friends that a deed had been done from which the country would not be able to recover for a long time, if ever ; and added, It has dropped a curtain between the present and the future, which to me is impenetrable ; and for the first time since I have been in public life I am unable to see the future. I also added, It has closed the first volume of our political history under the Constitution, and opened the second, and that no mortal could tell what would be written in it."

For many years, he had been the trusted leader of the South with regard to everything relating to slavery, though but a small band had kept pace with him. And in those portentous May days, when he, who had always rushed on in advance of all, the most radical of the

radical slavocracy, cried Halt! beware! all
dashed past him with indignant impatience, as
if he had been the last and most insignificant
among all the political apprentices. Now they
began to ask themselves whether he had not
after all been right. The day after the war bill
had been passed by the House of Representatives, Giddings had said : —

" We sought to extend and perpetuate slavery in a
peaceful manner by the annexation of Texas. Now
we are about to effect that object by war and conquest. . . . Now I say to those gentlemen who are
so zealous for this conquest that our slave States will
be the last to consent to the annexation of *free* States
to this Union. I know that Southern men are now,
and have been, zealous in bringing on this war and
for extending our territory; but they will, at no distant day, view the subject in its true light, and will
change their position, and will oppose the extension
of our territory in any direction, unless slavery be
also extended."

As soon as the words " territorial acquisitions " were officially pronounced, the verifica-
tion of this prediction began. The din of war
on the Mexican battlefields was almost drowned
by the vociferous passion with which the vic-
tors quarrelled over the expected spoils of the
vanquished. The Southern President, acting in
perfect unison with the slavocracy, had not

been disappointed in the expectation that the bloody flag, which he had dug out of the graves of the Spanish *conquistadores*, could be carried to the shores of the Pacific with the hearty approval of the North. But had he quite forgotten that it was absolutely impossible to make any conquest simply for the *Union?* The United States had ceased long ago to be a Union merely of *States;* they were above all a Union of two heterogeneous *sections.* There was not a foot of Union territory which was not the legal domain of one or other of these two sections, and much less could an inch of new territory be acquired without legally assigning it to one or other of them. And now a stanch Democrat and an ardent supporter of the annexation of Texas met the intimation that new territory was to be acquired with the demand that the South should be at once legally excluded from all participation in the fruits of the common exertions. The South would not and could not submit to that, for it was not only not fair, but it was the death sentence of slavery. The balance of power between the two sections would be irretrievably destroyed, and that in itself would be the death-knell of the " peculiar institution." And did the past history of the slavery conflict admit any doubt that the slavocracy would resist its doom to the knife ? On the other hand, how-

ever, was it likely that the North would yield,
if a man of the antecedents of Mr. Wilmot demanded such a proviso?

Every day brought new proofs how true Calhoun's prediction had been, that in the North
the future belonged to the spirit of abolitionism.
Just now it had received by the annexation of
Texas a more powerful impetus than ever before, and the South undertook to force the
North into a concession, in comparison with
which all the other demands of the slavocracy
were as nothing. Mexico had abolished slavery long ago. To allow the South to carry its
" peculiar institution " into a part of the conquered territory was therefore nothing less than
slavery propagandism with powder and lead.
The Northern freemen were to allow millions of
dollars, which they had earned with the sweat
of their brows, to be spent, and the blood of
their sons and of the Mexican patriots to be
spilled like water, in order to open a new field
of activity to the slave-driver's whip on a soil
which was consecrated to universal liberty and
legally protected against pollution by the tread
of a slave. Were the descendants of the Revolutionary patriots willing to present the world
with such a commentary on the Declaration of
Independence, and to hide their faces in shame
before the semi-barbarians of Mexico? Thus

the story of the treasure-digger, in whose hand
the gold turned into glowing coals, had become
true ; but, unlike that fabled personage, who
threw down the present of the evil spirit with
a curse, the United States had to keep at least
a part of their conquests. It was folly to expect that a war which, under false pretexts, had
been undertaken for the purpose of making certain territorial acquisitions would, under any
circumstances, be terminated by the administration and the majority of Congress without
securing any compensation, after more territory
than they had ever coveted had been actually
conquered.

Here was a mass of difficulties boiling and
seething in the caldron of the Mexican war,
which was beyond the skill of any political cook.
Perhaps some means could be discovered to let
the steam escape, so that no explosion would
ensue, but nothing could prevent the gradual
corrosion of all the rivets by the poisonous
fumes. Ardent Northern patriots helped the
President to cover the whole width of the continent with the folds of the star-spangled banner,
and thereby rendered the temporary destruction
of the Union inevitable ; hot-headed slavocrats
sustained Polk's policy and urged him on, in
order to realize the prediction of Henry A.
Wise, that the "peculiar institution" would

irresistibly press on, until the waves of the Pacific put a stop to its conquering march; and thereby they sealed the fate of slavery.

Calhoun acknowledged that he was "unable to see the future," and that he did not know what the second volume of the history of the United States under the Constitution would contain. If he had probed his own mind to the bottom, he would have been forced to add that he was glad of it. He would have shut his eyes with a shudder, if they could have pierced through the mist, for a voice, which nothing could silence, constantly whispered into his ear that it covered an unfathomable abyss. Now and then he tried to ease his heavy mind by reminding the South how earnestly and persistently he had raised his warning voice. But that could bring no comfort either to himself or others. On the contrary, his reproaches were met by the charge that he more than anybody else was responsible for the war, because it was the legitimate or even unavoidable consequence of the annexation of Texas. With hot indignation he repelled the charge as an absurd calumny; for the annexation of Texas had been an imperative patriotic duty towards the Union, and he had been willing to meet Mexico with regard to the boundary question in a most conciliatory and liberal spirit.

The latter assertion was probably true, but was it thereby proved that Benton's accusation had absolutely nothing to rest upon? Let it be granted, for argument's sake, that he would have come to an amicable understanding with Mexico, had it been certain or even likely that the unravelling of this snarl would be left to his discretion. The war was the legitimate consequence of the annexation, though it might have been prevented if the helm had remained in his hands. He had taught the people that it was not only right, but a national duty, to make territorial acquisitions, if the slavocracy declared its need of them for the safety of slavery, and that the stays of moral scruples might be loosened to almost any extent for this laudable purpose. *He*, therefore, had no right to blame Polk and the war party for anything, except that they were not satiated when he cried Halt! enough! They were over-zealous and maladroit disciples, but still they were his disciples. It was the old story: the wizard had called the spirits merely to prepare a bath, and his half-taught apprentices had them go on carrying water, till the house was flooded and destructive streams burst through every door and window.

But what was the use of these criminations and recriminations? What had been done could

not be undone. There the facts were, and they
had to be dealt with. Calhoun did not retire
to his tent like the irate Achilles. Just because
Polk's policy had led the slavocracy into a dangerous defile, it was all the more sure that the
shield and the spear of its veteran hero would
be seen at their wonted place in the thickest of
the fight. But to demand that he should now
simply step into the ranks of the administration
columns and obey the commands of their leader,
and to denounce him because he refused to do
so, was folly. Senator Turney, of Tennessee,
charged that he was prompted by his presidential aspirations to obstruct the passage of
bills necessary for the successful prosecution of
the war. Calhoun repelled the charge (February 12, 1847) with passionate indignation : " If
the senator speaks of me as an aspirant for the
presidency, he is entirely mistaken. I am no
aspirant, — never have been. I would turn on
my heel from the presidency, and he has uttered
a libel upon me. . . . No, sir. The whole volume of my life shows me to be above that."
We have seen that as to the past the facts
were pretty far from bearing out his self-lauda-
tory assertion, but as to the present the insulting intimation was indeed utterly unfounded.
It was a little too early after the last presidential
canvass for him to declare, " At my time of life

the presidency is nothing ; " but the history of that canvass had taught him that to indulge any longer in such aspirations would be folly, with a tinge of ridiculousness. Never again would he have permitted his name even to be mentioned as a candidate. And even if he had not understood the lessons of that canvass as well as he did, he would have scorned every temptation, at this critical juncture of affairs, to allow his course to be in the least influenced by any personal considerations.

On the other hand, it is easily to be understood how the war party came to suspect him of personal motives. He was so deeply convinced that the war was a blunder and a calamity that he allowed once more the doctrinarian bent of his mind to get the better of his cool practical judgment. Turney had been provoked into his accusation by a speech, in which Calhoun had very elaborately advocated the policy of a "defensive line." The active military operations were to be entirely stopped. The United States should confine themselves to holding the conquered territory on a certain line, quietly waiting for Mexico to make up her mind to come to terms on this basis. This he declared to be "the policy best calculated to bring the war . . . with *certainty* to a successful termination, and that with the least sac-

rifice of men and money, and with the least
hazard of disastrous consequences and loss of
standing and reputation to the country." The
difficulties which the enormous distances, the
climate, and above all the obstinate patriotic
pride of the Mexicans opposed to a successful
termination of the war, in spite of the brilliant
achievements of the American arms, were so
great, that one can understand how a clever
man could hit upon this strange plan, which to-
day must appear simply absurd to everybody
who is not acquainted with all the details of
those countless embarrassments. Nevertheless,
though the idea certainly could not stand the
test of a sober and somewhat close examination, yet if the partisans of the administration
had been familiar with what had occurred behind the curtain, they would have felt less
tempted to ridicule it, and to give it a slight
coloring of that " moral treason " with which
they charged all the opponents of the war. The
President himself had been in favor of this
strange project of the " defensive line." The
original draft of his message had recommended
it to Congress. Calhoun had known this ; but
he had not been informed of the alteration
which Polk had made at the instigation of Benton, who had convinced him that such a passive
policy of " masterly inactivity " was utterly in-

compatible with the genius of the American
people.

This was so true that probably neither Congress nor the people would have hesitated one
moment to reject the proposition as not only inexpedient, but also pusillanimous and derogatory to the national honor, even if the administration had supported it with all its influence.
As the personal opinion of a single senator,
it was, therefore, of no consequence whatever.
The majority could have afforded very well to
pass it over with a few indifferent remarks, and
consideration for the man as well as policy ought
to have advised such a course. With regard
to the main question, Calhoun had announced
in the same speech his complete acquiescence in
the unalterable facts : —

" It would be vain to expect that we could prevent
our people from penetrating into California. . . .
Even before our present difficulties with Mexico, the
process had begun. Under such circumstances, to
make peace with Mexico, without acquiring a considerable portion, at least, of this uninhabited region, would
lay the foundation of new troubles and subject us to
the hazard of new conflicts. . . . But it is not only in
reference to a permanent peace with Mexico that it
is desirable that this vast uninhabited region should
pass into our possession. High considerations connected with civilization and commerce make it no less

so. We alone can people it with an industrious and civilized race, which can develop its resources, and add a new and extensive region to the domain of commerce and civilization."

Once admitted that extensive territorial acquisitions had become inevitable, the other question, how they should be disposed of with regard to slavery, had also to be met directly. If Calhoun did not at once give a full answer to it, his delay did not arise from any desire to conceal his views. The object of his speech was to recommend the "defensive line," and for that purpose it sufficed to say how the territory to be acquired should not be disposed of. That he did with great emphasis : —

" We are told — and I fear that appearances justify it — that all parties in the non-slave-holding States are united in the determination that they shall have the exclusive benefit and monopoly ; that such provisions shall be made by treaty or law as to exclude all who hold slaves in the South from emigrating with their property into the acquired country. . . . Be assured, if there be stern determination on their part to exclude us, there will be determination still sterner on ours not to be excluded."

" This known pointed division of opinion " as to the ultimate disposition of the territory seemed to him to render the vigorous prosecution of the war impossible : —

"Now, if I may judge from what has been declared on this floor, from what I hear on all sides, the members from the non-slave-holding States, if they were sure that slavery would not be excluded from the acquired territory, would be decidedly opposed to what they call vigorous prosecution of the war, or the acquisition of a single foot of territory. Can they then believe that the members of the slave-holding States, on the opposite supposition, would not be equally opposed to the further prosecution of the war and the acquisition of territory?"

Ten days after the delivery of this speech, on February 19, 1847, Calhoun presented a set of resolutions to the Senate, covering the whole ground of the slave question with regard to the Territories. The key-note of the remarks with which he prefaced them was the assertion, that "the day that the balance between the two sections of the country . . . is destroyed is a day that will not be far removed from political revolution, anarchy, civil war, and widespread disaster." This was not intended as a threat, nor even as a warning, for he knew that it would not be heeded. It was simply the statement of the solemn conviction by which his course was determined. In his opinion he had been forced upon the position which he was about to assume. Adams's journal is documentary proof that he had not "always," as he now asserted, considered

the Missouri Compromise a surrender of the
"high principles of the Constitution." But it
was of little consequence when he had come to
that conviction. At all events, he now considered that compromise "a great error," and, in
spite of that, it had been at his suggestion, as
he informed the Senate, that the continuation
of the compromise line had been proposed in
the House of Representatives, as a settlement
of the controversy about the territory to be acquired from Mexico. He had not wanted the
Southern members to be "disturbers of this
Union." But the proposition had been twice
voted down by a decided majority ; therefore his
advice was now, "Let us have done with compromises. Let us go back and stand upon the
Constitution ! "

The resolutions affirmed : The Territories are
the common property of the several States com-
posing the Union. Congress has no right to
do any act whatever that shall directly, or by
its effects, deprive any State of its full and
equal right in any Territory : a law which
would prevent the citizens of certain States
from emigrating, with their property, into any
Territories would be such an act. Admission
of a State into the Union may not be made
dependent upon any other condition, except
that its Constitution shall be republican.

A refutation of this doctrine cannot here be attempted, for that would require a recapitulation of the whole slavery question and of the doctrine of state sovereignty. As to the question of constitutional law, it suffices here to say that, whether Calhoun was right or wrong, the whole history of the United States proved the assertion to be an absurdity; that what he claimed to be a "high constitutional right" of the slave-holders was "*not the less clear*" because deduced from the entire body of the instrument, and the nature of the subject to which it relates, instead of being specially provided for." If this "constitutional right" was as clear as if it had been specially provided for by the Constitution, then all the Southern statesmen, ever since the adoption of the Constitution, must have been utterly devoid of brains or absolutely nerveless, for the right had never been acknowledged or exercised. Calhoun himself opened "the second volume" of the history of the United States "under the Constitution," and, by his resolutions, he marked a new era, because they were not mere legal abstractions, but a political manifesto, announcing a revolutionary programme of fearful import.

"The Constitution which we now present is the result of a spirit of amity, and of that mutual deference and concession which the pe-

culiarity of our political situation rendered indispensable." Thus the framers of the Constitution had characterized their own work. North
and South had always declared with one voice
that the constitutional convention at Philadelphia would have labored in vain if the compromises concerning slavery had not been agreed
upon. Compromise had ever since been the
unsteady compass by which the course of the
Union ship had been directed in the slavery
question. To that, and to that alone, it was
due that the domain of slavery and the sway of
the slavocracy over the national politics had constantly increased. And now Calhoun demanded
that a heavy line should be drawn through this
word " compromise," and that it should for all
time to come remain expunged. It is true, he
only wanted " to go back and stand upon the
Constitution," but in the eyes of the North his
interpretation of it absolutely divested it of
the character of a compromise, and exacted the
unconditional surrender of the Union to the
slavocracy. Suppose he read the Constitution
correctly : that did not change the fact that it
was understood very differently by the North.

The Constitution in itself, however, was nothing but a dead piece of parchment, not even
able to resist the attacks of moths and mice.
There was no magical force in it, by which it

could of itself make known and enforce its true
will and intent. Like every other law, it became an active force only by the agency of the
people and their several constituted organs.
Whether right or wrong, that construction of
the Constitution had to prevail which the people
and their constituted organs believed to be
correct. Was it, then, possible that they would
ever adopt the doctrine of Calhoun's resolutions,
according to which slaves could be brought into
"any Territory of the United States, acquired
or to be acquired," and according to which, in
consequence, the slave-holders had been most
grievously wronged, ever since the establishment
of the Constitution, by excluding their human
chattels from all the Territories north of Mason
and Dixon's line?

The free States had by far the larger part of
the population of the Union, and they went on
steadily and rapidly gaining upon the South.
Many years ago, however, Calhoun had declared
with the utmost emphasis that, in the North,
the future inevitably belonged to the spirit of
abolitionism; and by this time the prediction
was so far fulfilled that, according to his own
testimony, all parties in the free States were
united in the determination to exclude slavery
from the territory to be acquired from Mexico.
The experience of the past certainly justified

the hope that it would be possible to break up
this unanimity, but would it ever be possible to
unite the majority of the whole people, irrespective of Congress, upon the basis of Calhoun's
claim?   The acknowledgment of this claim
would have been nothing less than the renunciation on the part of the Union of any policy
and will as to the future of its own political
nature; for the Territories were but inchoate
States, and experience had taught that, wherever slavery gained a firm foothold, it became
the paramount formative principle.   Calhoun
certainly believed in his own doctrine, but that
he should have expected ever to reconcile the
majority of the people to it seems hardly cred-
ible.   His idea probably was to obtain a good
deal by imperiously demanding all.   But he had
too carefully studied the history of the slavery
conflict not to know that, by thus demanding
all, the hatred of slavery and the opposition to
the slavocracy would be greatly intensified with
a very considerable portion of the Northern people.   The formation of a majority upon any
positive programme, therefore, evidently pre-
supposed the consolidation of the whole South
upon the slavery question, and the application
of very powerful levers to induce the rest of the
Northern people to support the slavocracy, in
spite of the prevailing current of public opinion
in their own section.

The framers of the Constitution had declared "the consolidation of the Union" to be "the greatest interest of every true American, in which is involved our prosperity, felicity, safety, perhaps our national existence." We have seen how ardently Calhoun professed the same faith in his earlier years. Now, he boldly proclaims the unrestrained expansion of slavery over all the Territories of the Union to be the shibboleth around which the whole South must rally.

"Henceforward, let all party distinction among us cease, so long as this aggression on our rights and our honor shall continue, on the part of the non-slaveholding States. Let us profit by the example of the abolition party, who, as small as they are, have acquired so much influence by the course they have pursued. As they make the destruction of our domestic institution the paramount question, so let us make, on our part, its safety the paramount question; let us regard every man as of our party who stands up in its defence, and every one as against us who does not, until aggression ceases."

That is the only means to save slavery and with it the Union. It is the only means, but it is also infallible.

"But if we should act as we ought, — if we, by our promptitude, energy, and unanimity, prove that we stand ready to defend our rights, and to maintain our perfect equality as members of the Union, be the con-

sequences what they may, and that the immediate
and necessary effect of courting abolition votes, by
either party, would be to lose ours, — a very different
result would certainly follow.   That large portion of
the non-slave-holding States who, although they consider slavery as an evil, are not disposed to violate the
Constitution, and much less to endanger its overthrow,
and with it the Union itself, would take sides with us
against our assailants; while the sound portion, who
are already with us, would rally to the rescue.   The
necessary effect would be, that the party leaders and
their followers, who expect to secure the presidential
election by the aid of the abolitionists, seeing their
hopes blasted by the loss of our votes, would drop
their courtship, and leave the party, reduced to insignificance, with scorn.   The end would be, should we
act in the manner indicated, the rally of a new party
in the non-slave-holding States, more powerful than
either of the old, who, on this great question, would
be faithful to all the compromises and obligations of
the Constitution; and who, by uniting with us, would
put a final stop to the further agitation of this dangerous question."

In truth, he was no novice in all the arts and
artifices of party politics.   How well he was
acquainted with the most sterling political quality of the Northern people, their unfaltering
loyalty and their religious respect for the law,
and how well he knew how to make use of that
for his purposes !   Still better was he acquainted

with the doughty character of the professional Northern politician, and he knew more thoroughly how to profit by it for the benefit of the slavocracy. But there was still the old mistake in his calculation, which vitiated it from one end to the other. The more unanswerably he proved the irrepressible character of the conflict between slavery and liberty, and the more violently he pushed it to its climax, so much the more closely he shut his eyes to the fact that slavery *and* the Union could *not* be saved, and so much the more loudly he cried that this *could* and *would* be done. He was only too successful in the consolidation of the South, and the effect of that upon the Northern politicians probably surpassed his own expectations. The slavocracy achieved triumphs, in comparison with which all its former victories appeared almost ridiculously insignificant. But all these triumphs only hastened the last inevitable consequence of the consolidation of the South, namely, the corresponding consolidation of the North. The perfecting of the consolidation of the two sections upon the slavery issue, however, *was* the breaking up of the Union.

The left wing of the Northern Democrats, which used to be called "Copperheads," throws the moral responsibility for the civil war upon the Republicans, because they forced the South into secession by forming a sectional party. This view of the case takes the symptom for the cause. The Union was not broken up because sectional parties had been formed, but sectional parties were formed because the Union had actually become sectionalized. The beginning of this process dated back to the constitutional convention at Philadelphia, and its roots were imbedded in the slavery compromises of the Constitution. The abolitionists — that is to say, the abolitionists proper, and not all whom Calhoun was pleased to call so — had been the first to recognize this fact, but they were not, properly speaking, a *political* party, because they refrained by principle from acting as such. The slavocracy was the first to proclaim the principle that the slavery issue must be the division line of the political parties. It did this with full consciousness of the import of the declaration; it carried the principle much farther than the Republicans did, until long after the beginning of the civil war; and Calhoun was in this respect, as in all others, the foremost leader of the slavocracy. The Republicans only opposed the extension of slavery. Calhoun, however, demanded that the South should unite in making the slavery question in all its forms and bearings the main plank of its political platform, and, in this shape, he wanted

" to force the issue upon the North." He writes
to a member of the Legislature of Alabama, " I
would even go one step farther, and say that it
is our duty — due to ourselves, to the Union,
and our political institutions — to *force* the issue on the North. . . . I would regard any compromise or adjustment of the [Wilmot] proviso,
or even its defeat, without meeting the danger
in its whole length and breadth, as very unfortunate for us. It would lull us to sleep again,
without removing the danger, or materially di-
minishing it." And how did he propose thus
to meet the danger? "There is and can be but
one remedy short of disunion, and that is to re-
taliate, on our part, by refusing to fulfil the stipulations in their favor, or such as we may select
as the most efficient." He proposed a convention of the Southern States, which should agree
that, until full justice should be rendered the
South, all the Southern ports should be closed
to the sea-going vessels of the North. The
northwestern States would be detached from
the northeastern by leaving open the trade by
river and railroad, and the northeastern States
would surely come to terms, for " their unbounded avarice would, in the end, control
them." To-day, the South knows whether the
avarice of the northeastern States is quite so
unbounded as Calhoun thought, and whether

the northwestern States are willing to let it depend upon the gracious good will of the South whether the national rivers, and especially the mouth of the Mississippi, shall be open to their trade.

One thing, however, Calhoun ought to have known already at that time, namely, that the North would never acknowledge such a measure to be a " retaliation." He said, " That the refusal on their part would justify us in refusing to fulfil those [stipulations of the national compact] in their favor is too clear to admit of argument." It was, in fact, too clear to admit of argument that, in the most essential point, the two cases had no more in common than yes and no. The opponents of slavery were convinced that Congress had the constitutional right, or even that it was in duty bound, to prevent slavery from entering the free territories to be acquired from Mexico ; and even Calhoun forbore to charge them directly with doing violence to their consciences and acting against their better knowledge. He, on the contrary, unreservedly acknowledged that he intended to deprive the North of its *constitutional* rights.

Benton very correctly said that such a resolution on the part of the South *was* the breaking up of the Union ; and now, as before, there

were not lacking people who maintained that it
was this that Calhoun was aiming at. They
understood the man the less in proportion as the
crisis and catastrophe more nearly approached.
In the same letter, above quoted from, he said:

"This brings up the question, How can it [the dan-
ger] be so met, *without resorting to the dissolution of
the Union?* I say without its dissolution, for, in my
opinion, a high and sacred regard for the Constitution, as well as the dictates of wisdom, make it our
duty in this case, as well as all others, not to resort
to, or even to look to, that extreme remedy, until all
others have failed, and then only in defence of our
liberty and safety."

That he honestly and ardently wished the preservation of the Union is, indeed, as certain as
it is certain that his remedies had the effect of
sledge-hammer strokes. The consciousness of
weakness drove him to the desperate resolution
to burn the ship of compromise, which had carried the slavocracy so far, and to demand the
unconditional submission of the North. "We
are now stronger relatively than we shall be
hereafter, politically and morally." He thought
the last moment had come, when it was still
possible to chain down the North so absolutely
by positive law that slavery could scorn all the
assaults of the brutal facts and the spirit of the
times. In truth there never had been a time

when that could be done, and it grew every
day less possible to do it, because this growing
weakness of the slavocracy was no secret to the
North. The forging of new chains for the
Northern States made them feel more than ever
the weight of those which they already wore ;
and in shaking these, while listening to the complaints of the Southern States that their political and moral strength was irremediably on the
wane, they learned better to know their own
strength. The will and the ability of the North
grew to do what, in its opinion, every political
and moral consideration bade it do. The more
the South succeeded in chaining down the North
by positive law, the louder and the more ener-
getic the protest of the spirit of the times and
of the facts became. And had Calhoun quite
forgotten that many years ago he himself had
declared that the ultimate decision would be
given not by the law, but by the facts ? So far
from swinging the firebrand of sectional agitation without cause, and only to further secret
treacherous designs, as so many accused him of
doing, he now, as heretofore, shrunk back from
drawing the last conclusion from his own premises, because he would not believe that slavery
and the Union could not both be saved. With
every new contest, it became more apparent
that the curse resting upon slavery was, that

every new success of the slavocracy was another step towards the judgment and doom of the "peculiar institution." This curse, therefore, necessarily weighed most heavily upon the thoughts and the deeds of him who, in all the tremendous exertions of the slavocracy against the onslaughts of the spirit of the times and of the facts, proved himself to be alone "a host." With the consolidated South, he now drove the North from the battlefield of the Wilmot proviso, but the quiver on his back was almost empty, the bow in his hand was cracked, and the field proved to be a barren conquest, so that the ultimate effects of the victory were those of a crushing defeat.

Benton, in his "Thirty Years' View," lays great stress upon the fact that Calhoun never called up his resolutions to be acted upon by the Senate, because they had been received with general disfavor. It is hard to imagine how Benton, after witnessing the further development of the controversy, could still think that this afforded any reason for exultation. Calhoun continued to oppose, with the utmost energy, the giddy agitators of unbounded territorial aggrandizement, though the contemplated acquisitions lay so far to the South that the slavocracy would probably have been able to secure the prey for the "peculiar institution." When there seemed

to be some danger that it would be impossible
" to conquer peace " unless the whole Mexican
republic was taken possession of, he still advocated his "defensive line," and he sternly
put himself against Polk's recommendation of a
temporary military occupation of Yucatan. But
while he did his best to prevent the sea of difficulties, into which the Union had been thrown
by the craving for more land, from being agitated even more profoundly, he did not recede
one inch from the position which he had taken
with regard to the equal right of the Southern
States to all the Territories. He had refrained
from calling up his resolutions, but the number
of converts to his doctrines increased at such
a rate that the " abstractions " rapidly changed
into a positive programme.

A bill for the organization of the Oregon
Territory had been passed by the House of Representatives at the second session of the 29th
Congress. The Senate committee, to which the
bill was referred, moved to strike out the clause
which, in conformity with the provisional laws
enacted by the inhabitants of the Territory,
prohibited slavery. As this motion would have
led to endless debates, the bill was laid on
the table, and Oregon remained unorganized.
Benton asserts that the motion to strike out was
made at the instigation of Calhoun. However

James K Polk

that be, at all events the fate of the bill in the Senate lay in the announcement on the part of the South that Oregon, although lying entirely north of Mason and Dixon's line, should not without more ado be given up to the North, and the resistance was based upon the doctrine of Calhoun's resolutions.

When the subject was taken up again by the 30th Congress, it was openly avowed that slavery was not expected to gain a firm footing in these high latitudes. The South declared itself to be contending merely for the principle. To force upon the North the acknowledgment of the principle was, however, evidently an utterly hopeless undertaking. The slavocrats, Calhoun not excepted, knew that well enough, and they were not such doctrinaires as to risk their bones in charging windmills. Calhoun was undoubtedly thoroughly convinced of the soundness of his theories, but the practical aim and end of his struggle for the principle was to wring from the North acceptable concessions with regard to all present and future Territories which were sufficiently well adapted for slave labor. So far from receding from the position which he had taken in his resolutions, he now carried their doctrine to its last legitimate consequence by denying the binding force of the former compromises. In his speech of June 27,

1848, on the Oregon bill, he said of the Missouri Compromise : —

"A compromise line was adopted between the North and the South ; but it was done under circumstances which made it nowise obligatory on the latter. . . . The South has never given her sanction to it, or assented to the power it asserted. She was voted down, and has simply acquiesced in an arrangement which she has not had the power to reverse, and which she could not attempt to do without disturbing the peace and harmony of the Union, to which she has ever been averse."

Calhoun was too candid and daring a man, he had too much of the fanatic, and, above all, he understood this question too thoroughly to approve of the covering up and concealing of the depth of the antagonism which necessarily aggravated the evils. He shares with the abolitionists the merit of having always probed the wound to the bottom, without heeding in the least the protesting shrieks of the patient. The return of the left wing of the Northern Democrats into the service of the slavocracy was acknowledged by him with a gracious smile, but he spurned the cunning device which made the bitter morsel palatable to the peace - craving masses. As his immediate purposes were served by it, he of course received with satisfaction the announcement that the reintegration of the Democratic party could and should be effected upon the basis of his doctrine of "non-interference." But no blame rested upon him for the fact that it was a reunion over the bottomless chasm of a conscious falsehood, because the "non-interference" as understood by the Northern Democrats had nothing in common with the "non-interference" demanded by him and the Southern radicals, except the abandonment of the right to have a national policy with regard to slavery in the Territories. When Cass and Dickinson now proclaimed the doctrine of squatter sovereignty, the cudgel of his logic with a few strokes smashed into atoms the coarse and bold sophisms. Whatever of legislative powers the Legislatures or the inhabitants of the Territories had, was derived from an act of Congress. If, therefore, Congress had no right to take any action whatever in respect to the introduction of slavery into the Territories, the former evidently could do so much less. Calhoun called the doctrine of Dickinson and Cass "the most absurd of all the positions ever taken." "The first half dozen of squatters would become the sovereigns, with full dominion and sovereignty over them [the Territories] ; and the conquered people of New Mexico and California would become the sovereigns of the country, as soon as they became the Territories of the United States, vested

with the full right of excluding even their con-
querors."

Calhoun's own doctrine was certainly more
logical, and he was perfectly consistent in denying to Congress, to the territorial Legislatures,
and to the squatters, as well the right to establish slavery as the right to prohibit it. But
nevertheless his theory also had a logical hitch.
He claimed for the slave-holders the right to
bring their human chattels into all the Territories as a right *under* the Constitution, but he
did not dare to assert that the Constitution
established slavery either in the Territories or
anywhere else. It had, however, thus far been
universally acknowledged that, wherever slavery
existed, it was the creature of municipal law.
Whence, then, should slavery derive its legal
existence in Territories where it did not actually
exist, or where thus far it was even expressly
forbidden by law, as in New Mexico and California? Was it now to be denied that slavery
could only be the creature of positive, though
perhaps unwritten, law, — *i. e.*, was the right
to hold slaves in any Territory to be derived
from the law of nature? If so, by what process
of logic could this natural right be limited to
negroes, and even to negroes who were already
slaves in certain other places? This course led
no less to sheer absurdity than the doctrine of

squatter sovereignty; and yet there was no other course, unless the Constitution was to be construed to *establish* slavery in all the Territories.

Conclusive as this logical hitch in the "non-interference" doctrine was, it dwindled down into absolute insignificance, when compared with the political absurdity of the theory. Calhoun's doctrine made it a solemn constitutional duty of the United States government and of the American people to act as if the existence or non-existence of slavery in the Territories did not concern them in the least. If they could not help taking an interest in it, at least that interest had to be purely academical, as if the Territories had been situated on some distant planet. The question was not allowed to be a question at all. Yet the fact was that North and South were perfectly agreed in considering it *the* question, in comparison with which everything else was as nothing. Thus the theory and the facts clashed in a most ridiculous manner; and in such a conflict between theory and facts the former has always to yield, though it be written in giant letters and with living fire in the Constitution. No people with the least vestige of political vitality ever will or can turn their backs upon a question which they consider of paramount importance to their whole future, look at the sky and whistle, because the Constitution says that the matter must not be touched ever so lightly with a single finger. And if the Constitution does not say that in so many words, but only an endless string of hotly contested assertions, deductions, and conclusions leads to this result, then the sole effect will be that another huge monument of human folly has been erected.

Nothing shows in so drastic a light the fearful embarrassment into which the policy of terri-torial aggrandizement had thrown the country as the recommendation of a committee of the Senate to solve the problem by adopting this ostrich policy. On July 18, 1848, Mr. Clayton, with the consent of Calhoun, who was a member of the select committee, introduced a compromise bill, which acknowledged the provisional laws of Oregon " till the territorial Legislature could enact some law on the subject of slavery." New Mexico and California were to be organized as Territories by the appointment of a governor, secretary, and judges, to compose a temporary Legislature, " but without the power to legislate on the subject of slavery; thus placing that question beyond the power of the territorial Legislature, and resting the right to introduce or prohibit slavery in these two Territories on the Constitution, as the same should be ex-

pounded by the judges, with a right of appeal to
the Supreme Court of the United States. It
was thought that by this means Congress would
avoid the decision of this distracting question,
leaving it to be settled by the silent operation
of the Constitution itself."

By acquiescing in this arrangement, Calhoun
abandoned his position on the "rock" of the
Constitution, and took once more the old track
of compromises. No better proof can be exacted
that he had claimed all in order to get enough.
But this comparative moderation was not yet to
be rewarded. Even Democratic organs emphatically protested against "the cowardly conduct of
Congress in seeking to shove [the responsibility
of the decision] upon the Supreme Court." By
the Senate the bill was passed, but in the House
it was laid on the table, on motion of Alexander
H. Stephens. Calhoun was of course free to
climb again to the top round of the ladder of
principle, but his doing so could no longer produce the same effect as heretofore. He knew
this well enough, and his discomfiture was the
greater because a leading Southerner had felt
himself called upon to move the rejection of the
compromise. The consolidation of the South
on the basis of the slavery question had indeed
so far been effected that every Southerner
peremptorily demanded for his section some

share of the Mexican spoils; but the representatives of the South were very far from being agreed as to the arguments on which to rest the claims, or as to the means with which their realization should be attempted. Calhoun had yet one arrow left in his quiver, and he did not hesitate to take it out; but its point was broken off by Southern hands ere he could shoot it.

After a most tenacious resistance on the part of the Senate, the first session of the 30th Congress was brought to a close by the passage of the Oregon bill as it had come from the House; that is, with the exclusion of slavery. California and New Mexico, however, had remained unorganized. The rapid and most abnormal development of the former, in consequence of the discovery of gold, imperiously demanded that Congress should at last do its duty towards the newly acquired possession. From all sides the cry was raised that it was a shame and an inexcusable wrong to give up the Territory to anarchy, because Congress would not come to a decision on the slavery question. But there seemed to be little chance that the knot would be unravelled by this Congress at its second session. The South showed no more disposition to yield than before, and the North had good reason to hope that a decisive victory could be gained, if it but braced up its strength and persisted. California had as yet only two newspapers, and both declared that the population was unanimously of opinion that "the simple recognition of slavery" in the Territory would be the greatest misfortune. "The people of New Mexico, in convention assembled" at Santa Fé, sent a petition to Congress, emphatically asking protection against the introduction of slaves. Calhoun called the petition most impudent, and Westcott thought it an abuse of the right of petition. But that did not change the fact that, if the introduction of slaves into these Territories should be permitted, it would be done against the solemn protests of the inhabitants. Squatter sovereignty, however, was the utmost limit to which the Democratic politicians of the North could hope to lead their constituents in the service of the slavocracy. The determined opponents of the slave power, therefore, felt sufficiently elated to take the offensive. In the House of Representatives, several motions with a view to the abolition of the slave-trade, and even of slavery itself in the District of Columbia, were made, and it was with some difficulty that the more moderate of these attacks were repelled by the South.

These signs of the times appeared to Calhoun so ominous that he deemed it necessary to prove to the North by an extraordinary demonstration that in this question the South thought, and eventually would act, as one man. At his instigation, sixty-nine senators and representatives from the South met for deliberation on December 23, 1848, in the Senate chamber. A committee of fifteen was appointed, which appointed a sub-committee to draw up an address. When this sub-committee met, Calhoun submitted to it the draft of an " Address of the Southern Delegates in Congress to their Constituents." Of its object the address itself said that it " is to give you a clear, correct, but brief account of the whole series of aggressions and encroachments on your rights, with a statement of the dangers to which they expose you. Our object in making it is not to cause excitement, but to put you in full possession of all the facts and circumstances necessary to a full and just conception of a deep-seated disease, which threatens great danger to you and the whole body politic." It did not pretend to have any new facts or arguments to lay before the people. It was throughout the old story, which, in and out of Congress, had been repeated many thousand times. Nevertheless, a short recapitulation of it in calm but incisive and even bitter language could of course produce a great effect. Calhoun, however, did not

rely principally on that. The fact in itself,
that all the Southern members of Congress
united in addressing their constituents in such
a solemn form, was to make an overpowering
impression not only on the South, but also on
the North. Men of all parties believed that his
designs went much farther and were of much
darker complexion. The old charge was renewed that he was driving directly at a dissolution of the Union, and some of the accusers had
evidently some apprehension that this time he
might possibly succeed. So far as his wishes
were concerned, however, the suspicion was
now as unfounded as it had been on all former
occasions. The possibility — and, in his opinion, perhaps no more an improbable one — of
the withdrawal of the slave-holding States from
the Union, he kept steadily in view. There is
no question about that, for he had often declared it in express words, and he had not now
made the concession to his more moderate colleagues to conceal it in the least in the address.
As the address was to impress the people with
the gravity of the crisis, it was a matter of
course that this eventuality had to be pointed
to in a forcible manner. Nay, more. One of his
purposes undoubtedly was to prepare the South
for it, and to make the South equal to the emergency, if it should come to the worst. But a

calm and attentive perusal of the curious document cannot fail to satisfy every reader that
its main object was exactly to prevent this dire
eventuality from becoming an actuality.

The assertion that if the North was allowed
"to monopolize all the Territories" "she would
emancipate our slaves, under the color of an
amendment of the Constitution," and then the
white population would "change conditions"
with the slaves, absolutely excluded the possibility of submission, if all the Territories should
be closed to slavery by the verdict of the majority. "As the assailed you would stand justified by all laws, human and divine, in repel-
ling a blow so dangerous, without looking to
consequences, and to resort to all means necessary for that purpose." But, at the same time,
the address declared it probable that the calamity could still be averted by the South. "If
you become united, and prove yourselves to be
in earnest, the North will be brought to a
pause, and to a calculation of consequences;
and that may lead to a change of measures, and
the adoption of a course of policy that may
quietly and peaceably terminate this long conflict between the two sections." This expectation caused Calhoun to leave the last decisive
word unpronounced. He had no positive measures of any kind whatever to propose. The ad-

dress, so to speak, lacked an end. It was a long string of premises, which suddenly broke off without a conclusion. All the advice it had to give was, "We earnestly entreat you *to be united*, and for that purpose to adopt all necessary measures. Beyond this, we think it would not be proper to go at present."

On January 13, 1849, the sub-committee reported to the committee of fifteen. A long and animated debate ensued. The Whig members showed very little inclination to follow the lead of Calhoun, and they afterwards avowed that they had consented to help dig the mine only in order to pour water on his powder. The address was adopted with a majority of but one vote. Two days later, over eighty members of Congress met and deliberated with closed doors. Considerable excitement prevailed in Washington, for "many of the most intelligent men" believed, as Horace Mann wrote on the same day, that "Mr. Calhoun is resolved on a dissolution of the Union." They were mistaken. "We hope that, if you should unite with anything like unanimity, this may of itself apply a remedy to this deep-seated and dangerous disease; but if such should not be the case, the time will then have come for you to decide what course to adopt." This last paragraph of the address stated with perfect truthfulness what he intended. To unite the South, — that was his purpose, neither more nor less, — to unite the South for good or for evil, as the case might be. He "*hoped*" that the North would yield when it should be convinced, by the unanimity of the South, that "the refusal of justice" would be promptly followed by the dissolution of the Union. This calculation was not to be submitted to the test of facts. Washington's anxious expectations came *post festum.* The reception which the address had met from the committee had already proved that the South could not as yet be united on the slavery question in such a manner that thereby the Union could either be saved or destroyed. The attempt to form a Southern party had completely failed. The address was finally issued, but among the signatures were the names of only two Whigs, while even several Democrats had refused to sign it. The whole number of signatures was forty, just enough to save the movement from ridicule.

If the private correspondence of Calhoun should still exist, and some time see the light, we shall perhaps be authentically informed of the effect which this signal and probably unexpected defeat had on his mind. His public utterances contain no explicit answer to this question. But we can form a conception, probably nearly correct, of his frame of mind, if we direct our attention principally to what he did *not* say and do. Nothing betrays the least personal disappointment. There is left hardly a glimmering spark of the fire of ambition, which once burned so fiercely in his bosom, for he knows that he stands on the brink of the grave. He is wholly and exclusively devoted to the cause with which he has absolutely identified himself. As faithful and determined as ever, he stands at what he considers his post of duty, — of duty towards his section, and therefore also towards the Union. Every device calculated to hinder the North yet a little longer in securing a " monopoly " of all the Territories, or to open a new chance to the South, by means direct or indirect, could count upon his earnest support, provided it appeared to him not derogatory to the honor of the South, and to promise at least a postponement of the evil day, on which the balance of power would be irretrievably lost. Once (February 24, 1849) he had a sharp passage of arms with Webster on the question whether the Constitution extends of itself to the Territories, and it was one of the strangest incidents in the strange story of the slavery conflict and states-rightism, to see the affirmative of this proposition sustained by the " great nullifier " against the great " defender of the Constitution." Upon the whole, he unquestionably got the better of his antagonist in this contest, which, short as it was, fully proved that his mental vigor was absolutely unimpaired. Yet a certain languor had evidently taken possession of him. The last weeks of the 30th Congress were the stormiest of Polk's stormy administration, but Calhoun refrained from increasing the excitement by a set speech. He had nothing new either to say or to propose. Too deeply was he convinced of the justice of his cause to despair of its ultimate triumph; but care sat heavily on his brow, for nothing would silence the voice which night and day whispered the maddening question into his ear, How is this all to end? Every day he found himself less able to answer the problem. Yet there was no halting; for something must be done, and he had become thoroughly convinced that nothing more was to be expected from Congress, unless an irresistible pressure from outside was brought to bear upon it. The time had come to write the omitted end of the "Address of the Southern Delegates in Congress to their Constituents," — to draw the practical conclusion from the premises therein enunciated.

The public did not know what share he had in the new movement. Even a leading politician like Henry S. Foote had no knowledge of it, though he himself was one of the principal instruments in the hands of Calhoun. So late as February 8, 1850, Foote indignantly rebuked Senator Houston for intimating that "the sovereign State of Mississippi, in the incipient movement towards the Nashville Convention, . . . was instigated by South Carolina, or her statesmen." And he added, "I know that what he has said will be understood as intimating, at least, that this Conventional movement of ours was stimulated by South Carolina, and was the result of concert between certain South Carolina politicians and certain politicians in Mississippi, with a view of having that movement originate in the State of Mississippi instead of South Carolina, in order to avoid any odium that might thereby arise. I am sure he did not intend to be so understood, and yet he will be, if he does not correct his remarks." Mr. Houston replied, "I can assure the honorable senator that this is a very delicate and complicated question. But I believe that if South Carolina had never existed, and if it had not been for her disposition and the movement which began there, Mississippi would never have thought of it." The senator from Texas probably was not himself fully aware at the time how true this assertion was. In December, 1851, Foote had to retract his former passionate and haughty disclaimer, and to excuse himself by stating that, at that time, " I did not believe that any human being in the world had received a letter from Mr. Calhoun on the subject, except one which I myself received." He now had to avow not only that Calhoun had "had a pretty extensive correspondence with persons" in Mississippi, but also that his (Foote's) mind had become satisfied by the perusal of these letters " that the *modus operandi* of the Convention was more or less marked out by his great intellect." Nay, he even declared with considerable pride, " It was through me, in the first instance, that Mr. Calhoun succeeded in instigating the incipient movements in Mississippi, which led to the calling of the Nashville Convention."

Foote, in the above-quoted rejoinder to Mr. Houston, has stated correctly the reason which prompted Calhoun to assign the part of ostensible leader to Mississippi, and which made him so anxious not to let anybody see that his hand held and pulled all the wires. The best proof of the consummate skill with which he played his game is the fact that even the chief actors had not the slightest suspicion of their being but tools in his hands. The details of the intrigue are not likely ever to be unveiled, because the greatest part of that secret correspondence is probably no more in existence. The loss is, however, of comparatively little importance, as one of those letters, — dated July 9, 1849, and addressed to Collin S. Tarpley, of Mississippi, — which came to light some time after his death, fully informs us about his intentions. He says : —

"In my opinion there is but one thing that holds out the promise of saving both ourselves and the Union, and that is a Southern convention ; and that, if much longer delayed, cannot. It ought to have been held this fall, and ought not to be delayed beyond another year. All our movements ought to look to that result. For that purpose, every Southern State ought to be organized with a central committee, and one in each county. Ours is already. It is indispensable to produce concert and prompt action. In the mean time, firm and resolute resolutions ought to be adopted by yours, and such meetings as may take place before the assembling of the Legislatures in the fall. They, when they meet, ought to take up the subject in the most solemn and impressive manner.

"The great object of a Southern convention should be to put forth, in a solemn manner, the causes of our grievances in an address to the other States, and to admonish them, in a solemn manner, as to the consequences which must follow, if they should not be redressed, and to take measures preparatory to it, in case they should not be. The call should be ad-

dressed to all those who are desirous to save the
Union and our institutions, and who, in the alternative, should it be forced on us, of submission or dis-
solving the partnership, would prefer the latter.

" No State could better take the lead in this *conservative* movement than yours. It is destined to be
the greatest of sufferers if the abolitionists should
succeed ; and I am not certain but by the time your
convention meets, or at farthest your Legislature,
that the time will have come to make the call."

It is the old programme ; only the way of
executing it is somewhat changed, and changed
exactly in the manner which he had repeatedly
pointed out in his speeches and addresses. It
was another attempt to save the Union, but, at
the same time, another step forward towards
its final dissolution, if the North should persist
in rejecting the conditions of the South. Calhoun's last great speech in the Senate proves
that he had not intended the Nashville Convention to present an *ultimatum* to the North,
though, for greater effect, he had perhaps
wished to see its propositions clad in the most
peremptory language. Whether or not he would
have liked to come at once to " an end with terror " rather than to endure still longer " the
terror without end," he knew that the South
was not yet ready to act. Therefore he did not
expect from the Nashville Convention what the

faint-hearted and weak-kneed peace fanatics of
the North apprehended from it, and it was very
far from fulfilling even what he expected. He
did not live to drink this new cup of bitterness, but he lived long enough not to derive
any consolation from the vain hope that this
last attempt to save the Union by rendering
slavery absolutely safe *in the Union* would be
successful. His eyes were too keen not to see
the fast-accumulating indications that another
disappointment — more bitter than all the disappointments he had experienced heretofore —
was in store for him. His weary limbs longed
to stretch out and rest, but he knew only too·
well that so long as his mortal eyes saw the
light of the sun there was no rest for him. By
their very keenness, these eyes became his worst
tormentors.

How often had he told the country that, by
everything dear to man and making life worth
living, the South would be compelled to sever
its connection with the North, if its equal rights
in the Territories were not recognized! But he
had never ventured to assert that, if this were
done, the peace of the country could never
again be disturbed by the slavery question, because slavery would thereby be absolutely secured against all attacks. His arguments were
always presented in such an ingenious form

that to the blunt logic of many of his hearers
this would appear to be the self-evident conclusion; but though he certainly deceived himself
to some extent in this respect, he had never directly and expressly asserted the fact. On the
contrary, all his speeches were replete with irrefutable arguments, proving that the slavery
question could not be decreed out of existence,
because the moral, economical, and political antagonism between slavery and freedom was a
fact, and would assert itself as a fact in all eter-
nity. The people, therefore, neither would nor
could acquiesce in it, if Congress should attempt
·to ignore it, or even forbid noticing it. No matter how high the "peculiar institution" was
placed on "the rock of the Constitution," the
waves of the sea of facts unceasingly beat against
it, and gradually washed it away.

In his great speech on the Oregon question
(March 16, 1846), Calhoun had said : —

"But I oppose war, not simply on the patriotic
ground of a citizen looking to the freedom and prosperity of his own country, but on still broader grounds,
as a friend of improvement, civilization, and progress.
Viewed in reference to them, at no period has it ever
been so desirable to preserve the general peace which
now blesses the world. Never in its history has a
period occurred so remarkable as that which has
elapsed since the termination of the great war in Eu-

rope with the battle of Waterloo, for the great advances made in all these particulars. Chemical and mechanical discoveries and inventions have multiplied beyond all former example, — adding, with their advance, to the comforts of life in a degree far greater and more universal than all that was ever known before. Civilization has, during the same period, spread its influence far and wide, and the general progress in knowledge, and its diffusion through all ranks of society, has outstripped all that has ever gone before it. The two great agents of the physical world have become subject to the will of man, and have been made subservient to his wants and enjoyments; I allude to steam and electricity, under whatever name the latter may be called. The former has overcome distance both on land and water, to an extent which former generations had not the least conception was possible. It has, in effect, reduced the Atlantic to half its former width, while, at the same time, it has added threefold to the rapidity of intercourse by land. Within the same period, electricity, the greatest and most diffuse of all known physical agents, has been made the instrument for the transmission of thought, I will not say with the rapidity of lightning, but by lightning itself. Magic wires are stretching themselves in all directions over the earth, and when their mystic meshes shall have been united and perfected our globe itself will become endowed with sensitiveness, so that whatever touches on any one point will be instantly felt on every other. All these improvements, all this increasing civilization, all the progress now

making, would be in a great measure arrested by a
war between us and Great Britain. As great as it is,
it is but the commencement, the dawn of a new civilization, more refined, more elevated, more intellectual,
more moral, than the present and all preceding it.
Shall it be we who shall incur the high responsibility
of retarding its advance ? "

Could he altogether refuse to see how much
the advance of this new civilization was re-
tarded by the " peculiar institution " ? The
most exaggerated eulogies on its conservative
virtues could not banish from his sight the
glaring contrasts between the two sections;
the most positive assertion that these were
wholly due to the unjust and unconstitutional
economical policy of the Federal government
could not conceal the fact that, no matter what
this policy was with regard to tariffs and internal improvements, these contrasts became more
glaring every year. No ingenuity, displayed in
the attempt to prove that the North would lose
infinitely more by a disruption of the Union
than the South, could disprove the fact that
these contrasts indicated the increasing weakness of the South, not only morally and politically, as he had himself avowed, but in every
respect; no prophecy that, after the breaking
up of the Union, the economical development
of the unfettered South would be unparalleled,

could cover up the fact that whatever touched any one point of the civilized part of the globe was instantly felt on every other, and that this economical, moral, and mental consolidation of the civilized world rendered the perpetuation of the " peculiar institution " impossible, because slavery, whether in itself good or bad, grew every day more incompatible with all the laws governing the life of this civilized world. Much duller eyes than his had begun long ago to be struck and alarmed by the fast-accumulating proofs of this all-important fact, furnished by the under-currents in the slave-holding States themselves. The non-slave-holders had begun to doubt the heretofore unquestioned identity of their interests with those of the slave-holders. In the border States the old creed was revived that slavery was a " mildew " and a " curse ; " in some of them an earnest agitation for its gradual extinction was entered upon. The old cotton States, and among them principally South Carolina, not only bitterly complained of the heavy drafts which the emigration as well to the northwestern as to the Mississippi States constantly made upon their wealth and their population, but they also saw the day approach on which a modified abolitionism would boldly raise its head actually among themselves, if nothing should be done to improve the miserable condition of their poor white people. But all the proposed remedies proved, upon closer examination, to be deadly poisons. The man who had been the zealous advocate of the first great Southern railroad, and who still bitterly accused the Federal government of having crippled the South economically, now gave it as his opinion that the South would commit suicide by introducing factories and stimulating all sorts of industrial pursuits, because the artisan and mechanic are born enemies of slavery.

All this could not shake in the least Calhoun's conviction that slavery was " a good, a positive good." But how could he have seen all this, and failed to perceive that, even if all the Territories were thrown open to the slave-holders, the " peculiar institution " would be as far as ever from being safely anchored in haven ? The future was still completely hidden from his view, and had forever to remain so ; for, as his theory of slavery had become with him a *dogma*, he was determined not to see it, and had become incapable of seeing it, unless he lived to see the dogma crushed by the accomplished facts. But he could not help seeing that the entanglements of the slavery question grew ever more labyrinthine, and he could not help feeling that the whole ground was thickly strewn with thorns.

Wearily he turned away from the facts, which he neither would nor could understand any more.

The 30th Congress had expired, leaving the question of the disposal of the newly acquired Territories where it had found it, and a Whig President had taken possession of the White House. Nine long months the people had to go about their business in this thick and sultry political atmosphere, ere their law-makers returned once more to the well-nigh hopeless task of solving this problem. Calhoun did not pass this time in idleness. The world of stubborn facts he had been unable to master, but he still thought himself able to prove on paper that he was nevertheless right. In these months, the " Disquisition on Government " and the " Discourse on the Constitution and Government of the United States " were in the main, if not entirely, penned. That he expected to exercise an influence on the decision of the impending question by these essays is hardly to be supposed. His idea seems rather to have been to leave an authentic exposition of his political creed as a political testament and solemn warning to posterity. At all events, it is only in this quality that they can claim a place in the history of the United States. Unlike so many of his speeches, they were not political deeds, and did not help to shape the course of events. Besides, when they appeared in print, he already rested in his grave, and every day the futility of the attempt to smooth down the wild breakers of realities by pouring on the oil of abstract theories became more apparent. To the student, these two essays will always remain among the most curious books of the political literature of the United States, and they may be read with great profit, though for the most part not exactly in the spirit intended by the author. The people have passed judgment on them without reading them; and have repudiated states-rightism, as Calhoun understood it, that is, state supremacy, as emphatically as they have repudiated the doctrine of the "positive good" of slavery.

When the 31st Congress met, December 3, 1849, the slavocracy was smarting under a defeat, the importance of which could not be overestimated. California, with the informal sanction of the President, but without any authorization from Congress, had adopted a state Constitution prohibiting slavery and involuntary servitude, and this clause had received the unanimous vote of the constitutional convention, although many of its members were Southerners. This was a commentary on the doctrine of the "positive good" of slavery which told more than all the abolition speeches ever made. California was irretrievably lost to the slavocracy, for to think that Congress could be compelled to force slavery upon her would have been sheer madness. Therefore it had become only the more necessary to struggle with the utmost energy for the rest of the Mexican booty, and for the principle, upon the acknowledgment of which those Territories which might be acquired at some future time could depend. The formal irregularities with which the proceedings in California were tainted furnished the South with a position of sufficient tactical strength to continue the struggle, with the hope that, after all, the strenuous exertions would be ultimately rewarded at least by a partial success. California was not to be admitted into the Union as a State until the North had made satisfactory concessions on all the other controverted points. At last, the slavocracy was apparently unanimous in the determination "to resist the aggressions of the North" to the last extremity. In the House of Representatives, the very same Southern Whigs who had so recently defeated Calhoun in his attempt to form a Southern party seemed ambitious to assume the leadership of the "fire-eaters." The gigantic edifice of the Union trembled to its very foundations, and, for a while, many patri-

ots hardly dared hope that its proud pillars
could be steadied once more. Week after week,
the storm of debate raged on with unabated
fury. Now and then the dark clouds were torn
by a compromise proposition, but in the next
moment they were again blown together by a
counter-blast, and the darkness seemed but the
greater for the passing ray of light.

No one watched the progress of the storm
with intenser interest than Calhoun, though
his voice had as yet hardly been heard at all in
the Senate hall. The hand of death lay heavily
on his shoulder. His body was sadly bent under its weight, so that the tears involuntarily
pressed into the eyes of those who remembered
what an image of strong and noble manhood
he had been. A dying man he was, though his
mental faculties were still unimpaired. But it
was not hope that fed the flickering flame of
his mind, so that it shone to the last in all its
original brightness. The knitted brows and
the deep lines, which care had chiselled into his
fleshless face, told with most impressive eloquence with what a heavy load he stepped into
his grave. Two years ago he had repelled
the charges of Mr. Turney with the proud assertion, " For many a long year, Mr. President,
I have aspired to an object far higher than the
presidency; that is, doing my duty under all

circumstances, in every trial, irrespective of parties, and without regard to friendships or enmities, but simply in reference to the prosperity of the country." The sense of duty was now the strong staff on which the expiring man leaned, and his iron will bade death stay its hand till he had done and the country had heard his parting words. Surely, he had a right to demand that the country should attentively listen to them. Now nobody could accuse him of being actuated by presidential aspirations, and his most embittered adversary could not dare to intimate that he was a fiend in human shape, who would willingly and wittingly kindle with his dying hand a fire which was to consume his country's peace, prosperity, and glory. Perhaps his political testament contained the best proof that what he had proclaimed to be white was black, and that what to him appeared black was white, but he certainly revealed in it his solemn conviction, and he could not have anything in view but what, in his innermost heart, he believed to be conducive to the true welfare of his country.

Calhoun had suffered for some time from an acute pulmonary affection, which had recently become aggravated by a heart disease. He himself was no more able to address the Senate for any length of time. On March 4, 1850, his carefully prepared speech was read by Mr. Mason, of Virginia, to the Senate. Every senator listened with profound attention and unfeigned emotion ; the galleries were hushed into the deepest silence by the extraordinary scene, which had something of the impressive solemnity of a funeral ceremony.

" I have, senators, believed from the first that the agitation of the subject of slavery would, if not prevented by some timely and effective measure, end in disunion." What a melancholy satisfaction for the man who, for nearly forty years, had been one of the brightest stars of the Federal government, in one capacity or another, thus to open his last speech ! He had contributed his full share to the glory and greatness of the republic, and now the last question which he had to argue in the Federal Capitol was, " How can the Union be preserved ? " Every line of the speech bears witness how thoroughly he himself is pervaded by the consciousness that it is " the greatest and the gravest question that can ever come under your consideration." Every word is carefully weighed ; not one syllable of angry and passionate declamation is to be found in it, — nothing that the most sensitive mind can construe into a threat. A " widely diffused and almost universal discontent " pervades the Southern States, caused by the belief " that they can-

not remain, as things now are, consistently with
honor and safety in the Union," because "the
equilibrium between the two sections . . . has
been destroyed," — these undeniable facts are
the basis of his argument.   He admits that if
this destruction of the equilibrium had been
" the operation of time, without the interference
of government, the South would have no reason
to complain ; " but he denies that such is the
fact.

The facts and assertions on which he based
this denial are familiar to us, and therefore
need not be repeated here.   Nor is it necessary
to recapitulate his version of the story of the
anti-slavery movement, and the reasons why this
hostility of the North to the "peculiar institution" would inevitably subject the Southern
States "to poverty, desolation, and wretchedness," after "all the power of the system " had
been concentrated in the Federal government,
and the North had " acquired a decided ascendency over every department of this government."
He declared "the views and feelings of the two
sections " in reference to slavery to be " as opposite and hostile as they can possibly be," and
he avowed once more that " all the elements of
influence on the part of the South are weaker,"
while " all the elements in favor of [the anti-sla-
very] agitation are stronger now than they were

in 1835, when it first commenced." He therefore asked, " Is it, then, not certain that, if something is not done to arrest it, the South will be forced to choose between abolition and secession ? " And he added, " Indeed, as events are now moving, it will not require the South to secede, in order to dissolve the Union. Agitation will of itself effect it, of which its past history furnishes abundant proof."

This startling assertion was probably deemed by many one of those wild exaggerations, verging upon the absurd, of which he had so often been guilty in the eyes of all the moderates and conservatives. Upon more mature reflection it could, however, not be denied that the split in several of the great religious denominations, to which he principally alluded, went far to warn the people that this opinion was not a daydream of the diseased imagination of a fanatic. Just now he proved, in a manner most unexpected to most of his hearers, that he judged the situation with more calmness and sobriety of mind than the great majority of them. " It is a great mistake," he said, " to suppose that disunion can be effected by a single blow. The cords which bound these States together in one common Union are far too numerous and powerful for that. Disunion must be the work of time. It is only through a long process, and successively, that the cords can be snapped, until the whole fabric falls asunder." The history of the next ten years decided in an unmistakable manner the question whether he was right, or those who thought that the 31st Congress would be the last of the old Union. At the same time, the sentences just quoted are proof absolute of the injustice of the accusation that Calhoun was consciously aiming at the dissolution of the Union, in order to become President of a part, since he could not become President of the whole. Even if he had been such a black traitor at heart, he knew that his foul designs could not be executed in time to gratify such a mad and petty ambition. Who can tell what "the second volume of the history of the United States under the Constitution" would contain, if the conservatives of the North had known as well as he knew how strong the Union was? He was no more thoroughly convinced of the inevitability of its disruption than of the impossibility to "snap the cords" in this moment and by one blow. And so far from wishing that it could or should be done, his last bequest to his country was an answer to the question how the Union could and should be saved.

Ere he proceeded to answer this question, he stated how it could not be done. "Nor can the plan proposed by the distinguished senator from

Kentucky [Henry Clay], nor that of the administration, save the Union." The course of events has proved the correctness of this opinion. Such compromises could postpone the evil day, but the catastrophe became only the more certain and terrible. No more could eulogies on the Union and appeals to Washington's warnings in his Farewell Address avert the danger. " The cry of ' Union, Union, — the glorious Union!' can no more prevent disunion than the cry of ' Health, health, — glorious health!' on the part of the physician, can save a patient lying dangerously ill." The only way to cure the disease was to remove its causes. Sure enough; but could that be done? He answered, " Yes, *easily;* not by the weaker party, for it can of itself do nothing, — not even protect itself, — but by the stronger. The North has only to will it to accomplish it; to do justice by conceding to the South an equal right in the acquired territory, and to do her duty by causing the stipulations relative to fugitive slaves to be faithfully fulfilled; to cease the agitation of the slavery question, and to provide for the insertion of a provision in the Constitution, by an amendment, which will restore to the South, in substance, the power she possessed of protecting herself, before the equilibrium between the sections was destroyed by the action of this government."

Now, if that was needed to save the Union, and nothing less would do, then the Union could not be saved.   For the first time, Calhoun directly asserted that, if the North would but follow his advice, " discontent will cease ; harmony and kind feelings between the sections be restored, and every apprehension of danger to the Union removed ; " and he followed up this assertion by demanding what was in the strictest sense of the word impossible.   The members of Congress from the North could not only concede to the South an equal right in the acquired territory, but even abandon it entirely to the slavocracy, and they could bid the people deliver fugitive slaves "with alacrity," as Webster afterwards did; but the North *could* not cease agitating the slave question, because it *could* not *will* it.   It *was* a *question*, as Calhoun himself had correctly called it, and it is a physical impossibility to *will* a great economical, moral, and political question out of existence ; and if it had not been physically impossible, the North could not have overcome the moral impossibility to will what it actually did not will; that is to say, she could not will to change or annihilate her economical, moral, and political convictions relative to slavery, — she could not will it, simply because they were convictions.

Nor is that all.   Calhoun did not say in

his speech how the Constitution ought to be amended, in order to restore and secure to the South, for all time to come, the lost equilibrium, but the answer to this question is to be found in the second of the above-mentioned essays. He had the candor there to admit that a constitutional amendment would in itself not be sufficient. The necessary preliminary step was to expunge from the statute-book all the laws by which the *Federal* Union of the Constitution had been changed into a *national* Union. Suppose this was granted: would the actual consolidation of the Union, with its nationalizing tendencies, which had been uninterruptedly going on ever since the adoption of the Constitution, be also wiped away thereby? Calhoun took good care not to propound this question. He confined himself to the statement that the lost equilibrium between the two sections could not be thus restored. But if it was impossible to undo what had been done, it was at least possible to prevent the sins of the past from having any practical effect in the future. This he proposed to do by giving to the weaker section " a negative on the action of the [Federal] government." He admitted that the government might thereby " lose something in promptitude of action," but he asserted that, " instead of being weakened," it would be " greatly strengthened," for it would "gain vastly in moral power." As the surest and simplest of the various ways in which the desired object could be effected, he recommended a reorganization of the executive power,

"so that its powers, instead of being vested, as they now are, in a single officer, should be vested in two; to be so elected that the two should be constituted as the special organs and representatives of the respective sections in the executive department of the government and requiring each to approve all the acts of Congress before they shall become laws. One might be charged with the administration of matters connected with the foreign relations of the country, and the other, of such as were connected with its domestic institutions; the selection to be decided by lot. . . . As no act of Congress could become a law without the assent of the chief magistrates representing both sections, each, in the elections, would choose the candidate who, in addition to being faithful to its interests, would best command the esteem and confidence of the other section. And thus the presidential election, instead of dividing the Union into hostile geographical parties, — the stronger struggling to enlarge its powers, and the weaker to defend its rights, as is now the case, — would become the means of restoring harmony and concord to the country and the government. It would make the Union a union in truth, a bond of mutual affection and brotherhood."

That was the "conservative principle" of nullification in its highest perfection, coupled with

the total abandonment of the Federal structure
on the basis of state sovereignty. The Constitution, as has been stated before, knew nothing
whatever of sections, and their actual formation
was in itself the first step towards the dissolution of the Union. The Union was endangered,
not because the original equilibrium between
the sections had been destroyed, but because,
by the agency of the slave question, it had been
actually split into two geographical sections, of
unequal strength. And now this fact, which
ran directly counter to the constitutive principle
of the Union, as established by the Constitution,
was to be made its determining principle ; that
is to say, the disease was to be cured by making
the cause of the disease the vital principle of
the body politic. Nothing, absolutely nothing,
was left of the equality of the States, which
was the basis of the states-rights doctrine, and
in a modified form also of the Constitution, if a
permanent minority of the States forming a geographical section had an absolute veto against
the majority in all Federal concerns. It was a
misnomer — nay, one might justly say, it was
a bold abuse of the name — still to speak of a
Union, if the constituent members of the commonwealth were to be constitutionally consolidated into a permanent geographical minority
and a permanent geographical majority, which,

in every question, had to come to a complete understanding, ere the body politic became capable of political action in any manner whatever. Calhoun's remedy, which was to effect the cure so "easily," was in fact nothing less than the actual dissolution of the Union, thinly covered by some artificial contrivances, which could not serve any purpose except to keep it for a little while mechanically together, and to expose it to the scorn and ridicule of the whole world.

"Having faithfully done my duty to the best of my ability, both to the Union and my section, throughout this agitation, I shall have the consolation, let what will come, that I am free from all responsibility." Those were the last words of the last speech of the great and honest nullifier. He could no more support himself. Two friends had to lead him out of the Senate chamber. Slowly and heavily the curtain rolled down to shut from the public gaze the last scene of the grand tragedy of this brilliant life. For nearly twenty years the suspicion and even the direct accusation had weighed on his shoulders, that he was systematically working at the destruction of the Union. By doing more than any other single man towards raising the slavocracy to the pinnacle of power, he had actually done more than any other man to hasten the catastrophe and to determine its character, and yet he labored to the last with the intense anxiety of the true patriot to avert the fearful calamity. But the last efforts of his powerful mind were a most overwhelming refutation of all the doctrines whose foremost champion he had been, ever since the days of nullification. It would have been impossible to pass a more annihilating judgment on them than he himself did in his speech of March 4, 1850, and in the Discourse on the Constitution. Yet he had been absolutely sincere in everything he had said. On March 5, in a short running debate with Mr. Foote, of Mississippi, he declared, "As things now stand, the Southern States cannot remain in the Union;" and a few minutes later he asserted, "If I am judged by my acts, I trust I shall be found as firm a friend of the Union as any man within it."

Calhoun closed this colloquy with the remark, "If any senator chooses to comment upon what I have said I trust I shall have health to defend my own position." This hope was not to be fulfilled, though he still spoke in the Senate as late as March 13, and in a manner, as Webster stated in his eulogy, "by no means indicating such a degree of physical weakness as did in fact possess him." On the last day of the month, the "magic wires" carried the tidings into every part of the Union that John Caldwell Calhoun was no more. To the last moment, he manifested the deepest interest and concern in the troubles of his country. "The South! The poor South! God knows what will become of her!" murmured his trembling lips; but he died with that serenity of mind which only a clear conscience can give on the death-bed. On February 12, 1847, he had said in the Senate, "If I know myself, if my head was at stake, I would do my duty, be the consequences what they might." It was his solemn conviction that throughout his life he had faithfully done his duty, both to the Union and to his section, because, as he honestly believed slavery to be "a good, a positive good," he had never been able to see that it was impossible to serve at the same time the Union and his section, if his section was considered as identical with the slavocracy. In perfect good faith he had undertaken what no man could accomplish, because it was a physical and moral impossibility: antagonistic principles cannot be united into a basis on which to rest a huge political fabric. Nullification and the government of law; state supremacy and a constitutional Union, endowed with the power necessary to minister to the wants of a great people; the nationalization of slavery upon the basis of states-rightism in a federal Union, composed principally of free

communities, by which slavery was considered
a sin and a curse; equality of States and constitutional consolidation of geographical sections, with an artificial preponderance granted
to the minority, — these were incompatibilities,
and no logical ingenuity could reason them together into the formative principle of a gigantic
commonwealth.   The speculations of the keenest political logician the United States had ever
had ended in the greatest logical monstrosity
imaginable, because his reasoning started from
a *contradictio in adjecto*.   This he failed to see,
because the mad delusion had wholly taken possession of his mind that in this age of steam and
electricity, of democratic ideas and the rights
of man, slavery was "the most solid foundation of liberty."   More than to any other man,
the South owed it to him that she succeeded
for such a long time in forcing the most democratic and the most progressive commonwealth
of the universe to bend its knees and do hom-
age to the idol of this "peculiar institution;"
but therefore also the largest share of the responsibility for what at last did come rests on
his shoulders.

No man can write the last chapter of his
own biography, in which the *Facit* of his whole
life is summed up, so to say, in one word.   If

ever a new edition of the works of the greatest
and purest of proslavery fanatics should be
published, it ought to have a short appendix,
— the emancipation proclamation of Abraham
Lincoln.

INDEX